The
Beatles

IN PICTURES

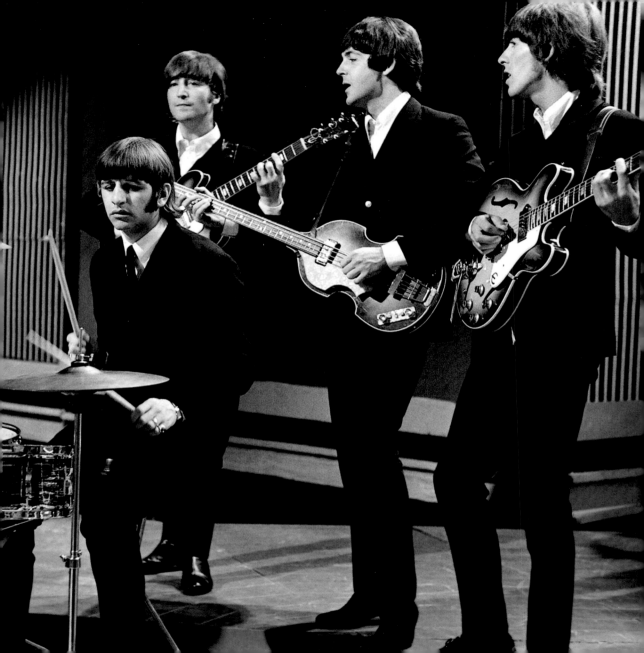

The Beatles

IN PICTURES

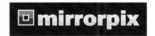

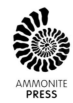

AMMONITE
PRESS

First published 2018 by
Ammonite Press
an imprint of Guild of Master Craftsman
Publications Ltd
Castle Place, 166 High Street, Lewes,
East Sussex, BN7 1XU, United Kingdom
www.ammonitepress.com

This hardback edition published 2024

Text © GMC Publications Ltd, 2018
Images © Mirrorpix, 2018
Copyright in the Work © GMC Publications Ltd, 2018

ISBN 978-1-78145-490-9

Publisher: Jason Hook
Editor: George Lewis
Series Editor: Richard Wiles
Design Manager: Robin Shields
Picture Research: Mirrorpix

Colour reproduction by GMC Reprographics
Printed and bound in China

Cover: The boys pose for a group portrait.
10 February 1963

Page 2: The Beatles on the set of *Top Of the Pops*, where they mimed to their latest No. 1, 'Paperback Writer'. This was not their first appearance on the BBC show, but it was their only live studio performance.
16 June 1966

Page 5: During a live TV performance only John and Paul were given microphones. Harrison shared with McCartney on a Lennon-led number.
c.1964

Page 6: A CBS photo call for The Ed Sullivan Show. Harrison is the only one not wearing a shirt-and-tie combination that was, until then, part of the standard Beatles rig.
8 February 1964

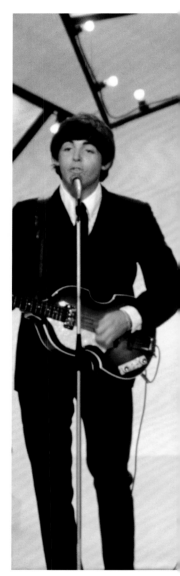

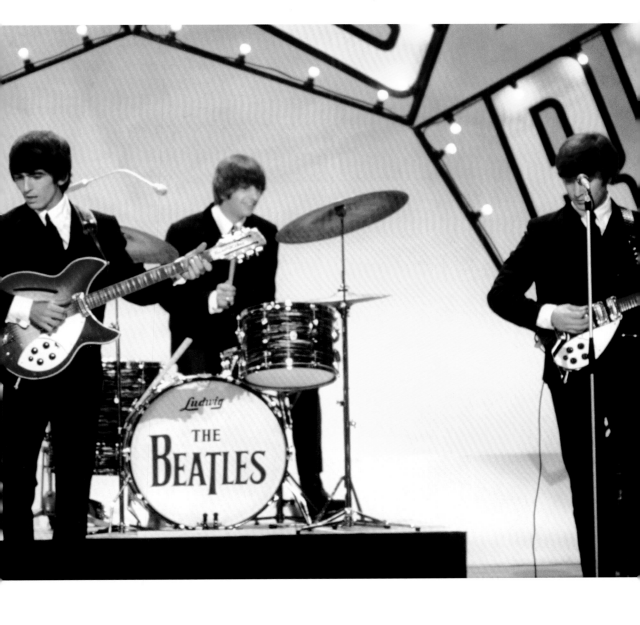

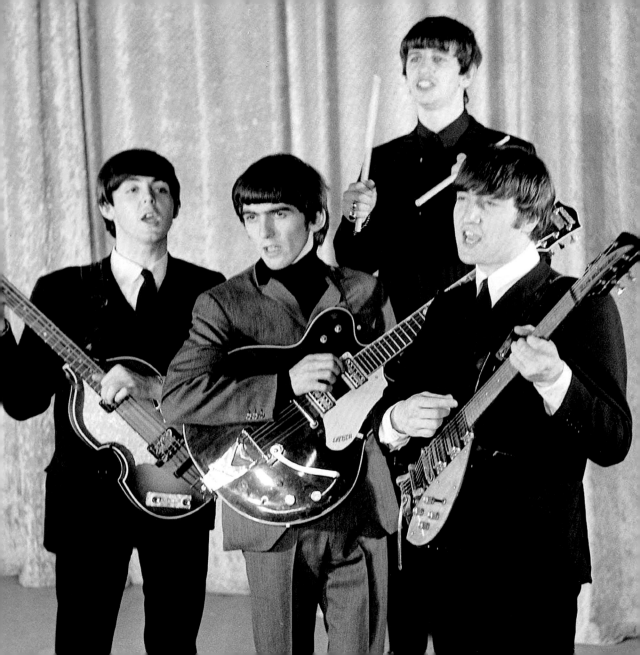

Introduction

The Beatles – John Lennon, Paul McCartney, George Harrison and Ringo Starr – came together in 1960 and broke up in 1970. When they first started, few people believed that pop music was anything more than a nine days' wonder, and it was thought that its shooting stars would soon fizzle out and land in the mundane blue-collar jobs they'd hoped to avoid.

But more than half a century later the form is still alive and well; and, for some, hugely profitable. Many luminaries of the early period are performing long after they qualified for old age pensions and several of them – including The Rolling Stones and The Who – have lasted long enough to make The Beatles' 10 years together seem almost ephemeral.

Yet, in that fairly short time, The Beatles stamped a deep impression on the Sixties, reflecting and often creating the zeitgeist. Of course, they were to some extent derivative: it's not hard to identify their musical roots in the recordings of Chuck Berry, Little Richard, Fats Domino, Elvis Presley, The Everly Brothers and Buddy Holly. But the Liverpool quartet were no mere imitators: they took the raw material of American rock 'n' roll and synthesized it into something unique and quintessentially British. More than that, they always resisted the classic temptation to just keep doing what they'd always done and hence ossify. They assimilated some of the outstanding qualities of contemporary rivals such as Smokey Robinson and Bob Dylan, all the while adding new original touches of their own.

And their music has endured, exerting a strong and unmistakable influence on each succeeding generation. It is starting to look as if The Beatles, like Shakespeare, were not of an age but for all time.

Success made the group members rich beyond their wildest dreams, but it was money that came between them and their split was acrimonious, with Lennon and McCartney ending up deeply mistrustful of each other's intentions.

Thereafter, the four pursued solo careers with varying degrees of success. For a while they tried to put The Beatles behind them, playing only new material. But they were no more able than anyone else to move beyond the group's shadow. Gradually they reached accommodation with their own past, and in live performance started to mix old material with new.

Today, it's hard to think of a band that does not owe something to the work of The Beatles; what's not so easy is to identify one that is quite as good.

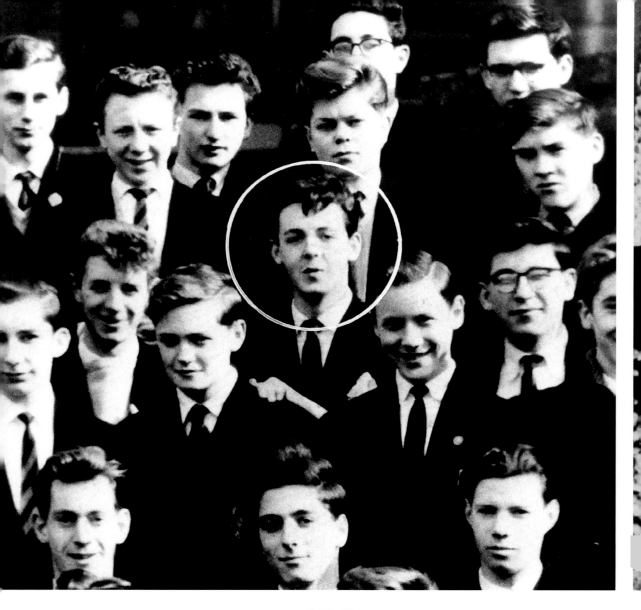

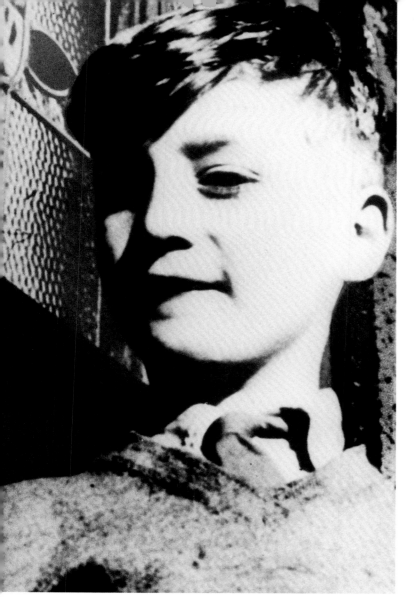

'I used to get mad at my school...'
Far left: Paul McCartney in a photograph at Liverpool Institute, which he attended from 1953 to 1960 and where he became friendly with an aspiring musician in the year below him, George Harrison.
1950s

Little Child
The young John Lennon looks bright and cheeky and perhaps constrained by the straight collar and tie: the child is father of the man.
c.1950

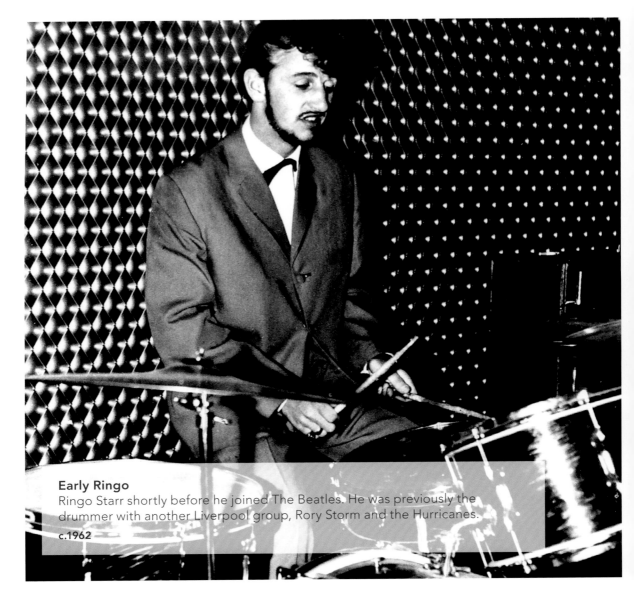

Early Ringo
Ringo Starr shortly before he joined The Beatles. He was previously the drummer with another Liverpool group, Rory Storm and the Hurricanes.
c.1962

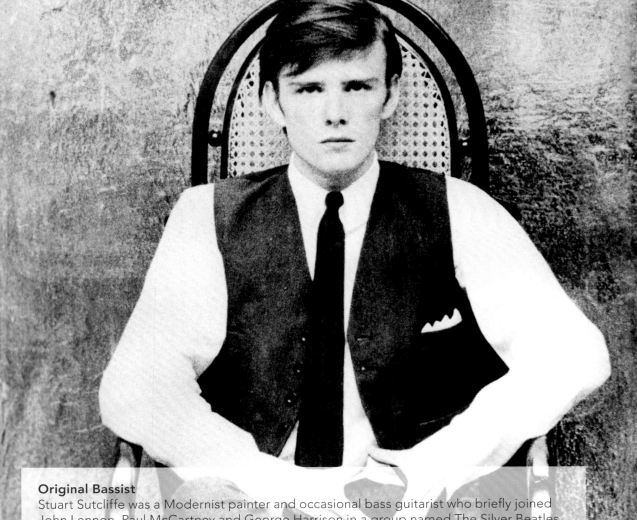

Original Bassist
Stuart Sutcliffe was a Modernist painter and occasional bass guitarist who briefly joined John Lennon, Paul McCartney and George Harrison in a group named The Silver Beatles.
pre-1962

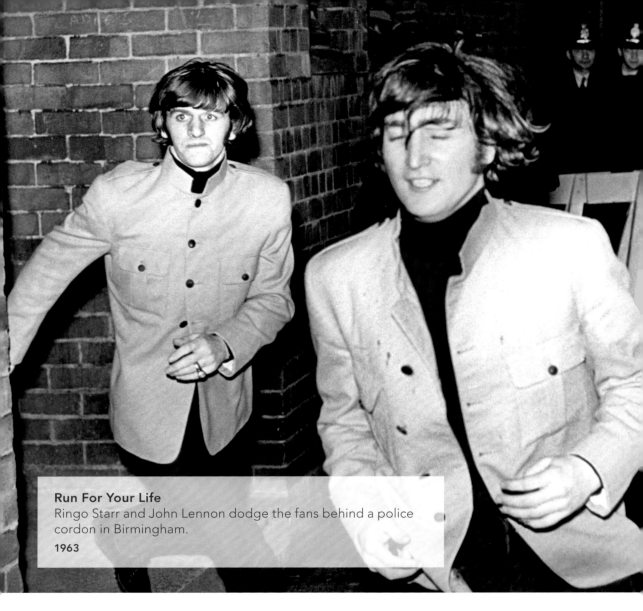

Run For Your Life
Ringo Starr and John Lennon dodge the fans behind a police cordon in Birmingham.

1963

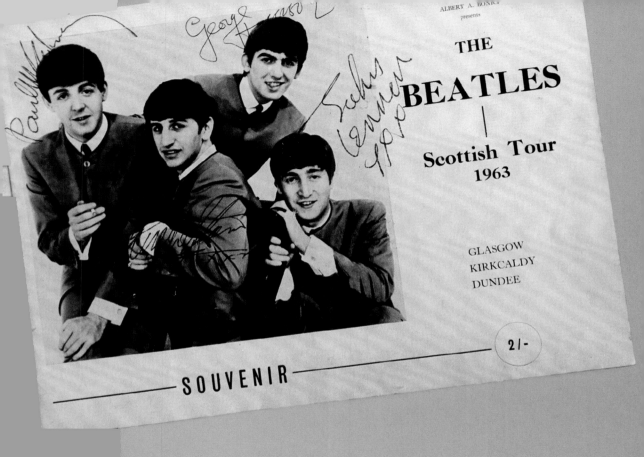

Braving Scotland
Signed souvenir programme from The Beatles' gigs at Glasgow, Kirkcaldy and Dundee on the 1963 tour of Scotland.
1963

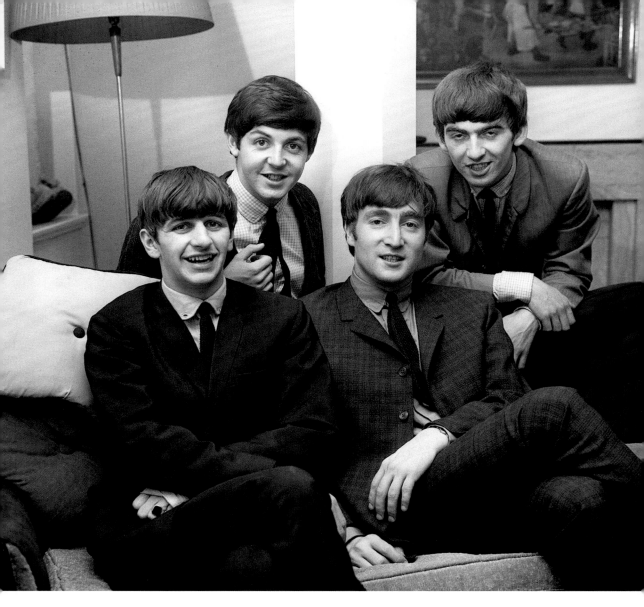

The Beatles

The Beatles At Home
Left: The Beatles at the home of *Daily Mirror* writer and showbiz biographer Donald Zec during an interview for a feature on the band.
Right: George smoulders while stirring his tea.

1963

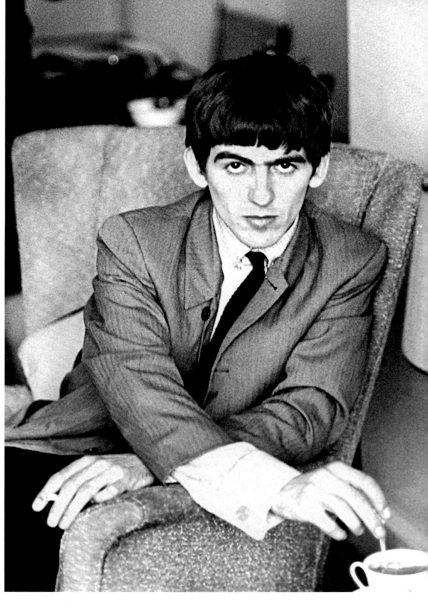

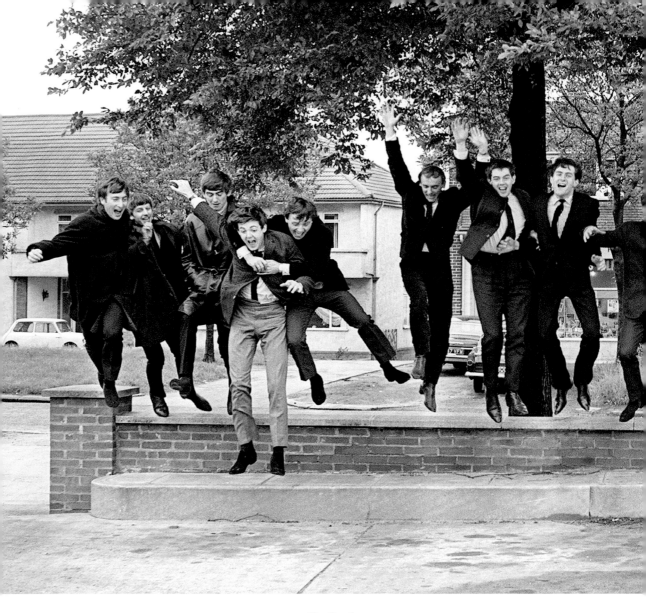

The Beatles

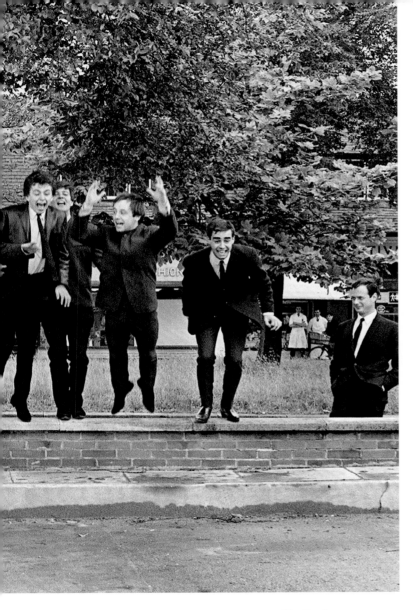

Off The Wall
Three leading pop groups
in their native Liverpool.
(L–R) The Beatles; Gerry and
The Pacemakers (with Gerry
Marsden holding on to Paul
McCartney); Billy J. Kramer
and The Dakotas (Kramer
partially concealed, fourth R).
Watching approvingly,
far right, is the manager of
all of them, Brian Epstein.
18 June 1963

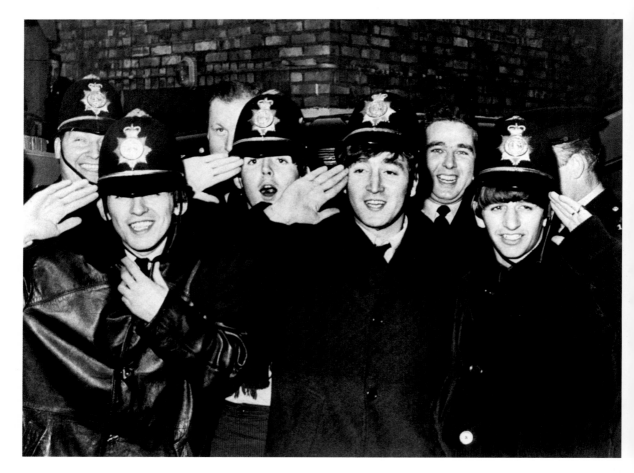

New Recruits

Impersonating police officers may be an offence, but you have more chance of getting away with it when you're a famous foursome and your current single – 'From Me To You' – is No. 1 in the Top 20.

10 June 1963

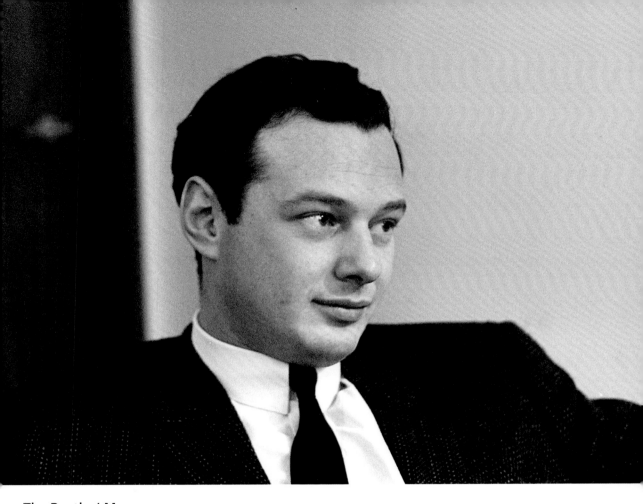

The Beatles' Manager

Brian Epstein was The Beatles' manager from 24 January 1962 until his death from an overdose of barbiturates on 27 August 1968. His influence on the group is hard to overestimate. As McCartney said: 'If anyone was the fifth Beatle, it was Brian.'

2 October 1963

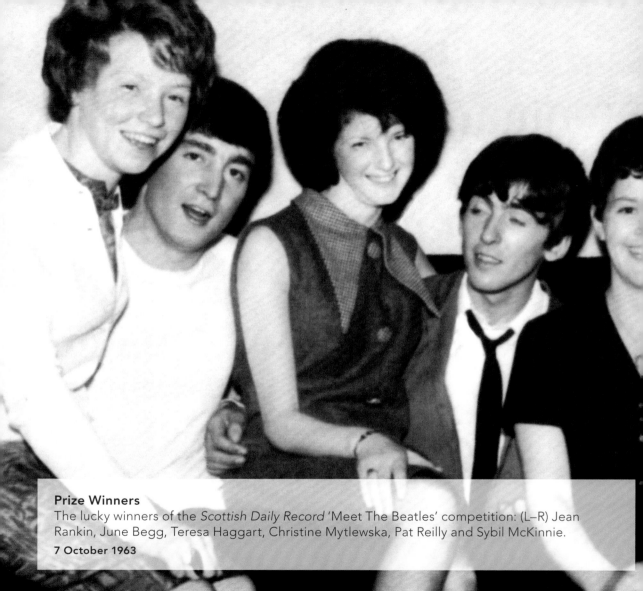

Prize Winners
The lucky winners of the *Scottish Daily Record* 'Meet The Beatles' competition: (L–R) Jean Rankin, June Begg, Teresa Haggart, Christine Mytlewska, Pat Reilly and Sybil McKinnie.
7 October 1963

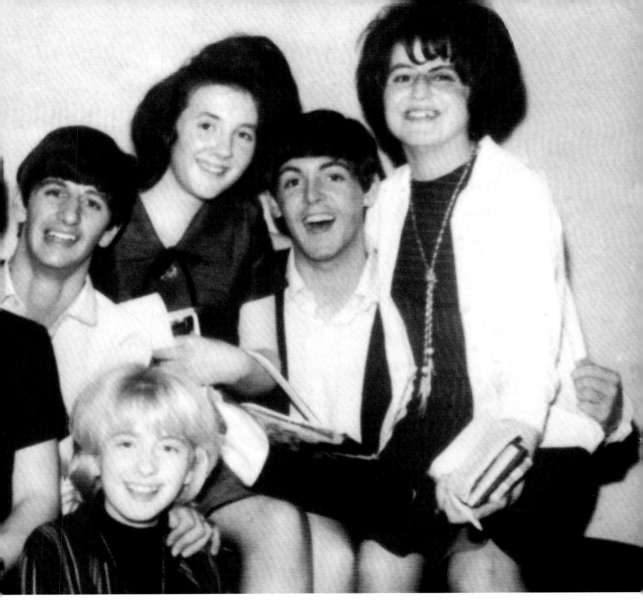

The Beatles

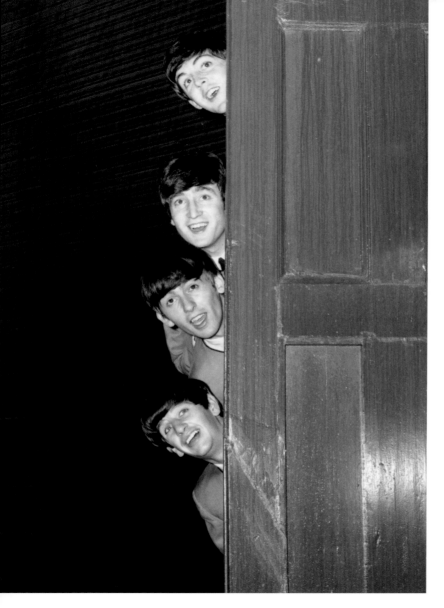

Television Stars

On ITV's *Sunday Night at the London Palladium*, the group's short set culminated in their current No. 1, 'She Loves You', and a rousing rendition of 'Twist and Shout'. Here the quartet pose for a pre-show photocall.

13 October 1963

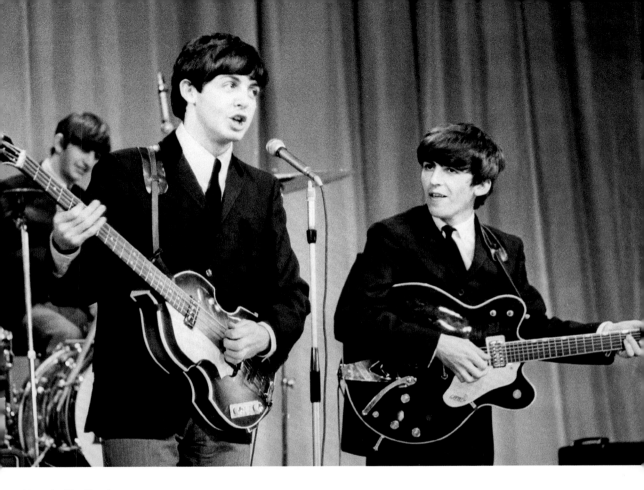

Ready To Rock
The Beatles on stage at the London Palladium on one of those
nights when everyone remembers where they were.

13 October 1963

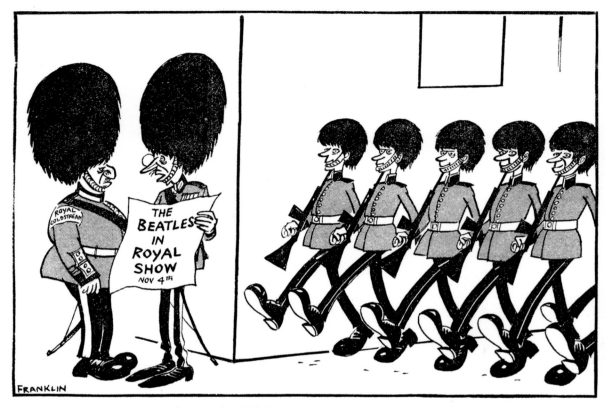

"GAD, SMITHERS, WHAT NEXT?"

Drawing Attention
News that The Beatles would appear at the 1963 Royal Command Performance inspired this cartoon by the *Daily Mirror*'s Stanley Franklin.

18 October 1963

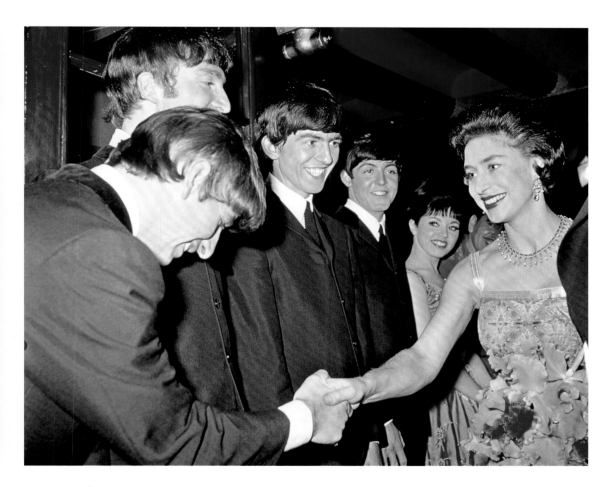

A Royal Meeting

The Beatles are presented to HRH Princess Margaret at the Royal Command Performance. The star-studded line-up also included Marlene Dietrich and Tommy Steele, but there is only one act that people remember.

4 November 1963

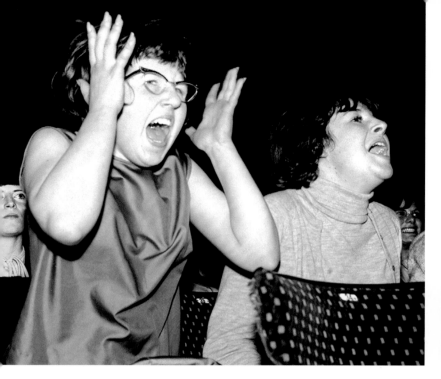

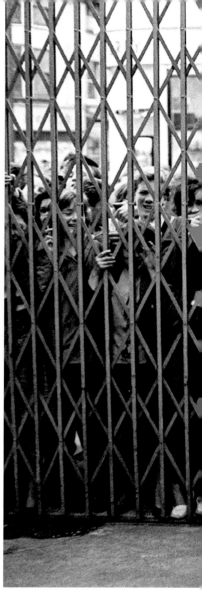

Beatlemania
Fans (particularly girls) would scream so loudly in the group's presence that it was sometimes impossible to hear what they were playing. The photograph shows the teens of Exeter, Devon, following a national trend that would shortly sweep the world.

November 1963

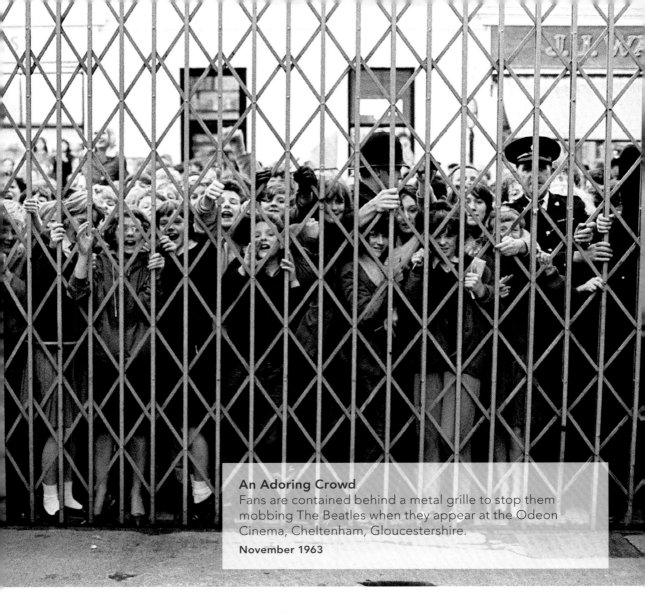

An Adoring Crowd
Fans are contained behind a metal grille to stop them mobbing The Beatles when they appear at the Odeon Cinema, Cheltenham, Gloucestershire.

November 1963

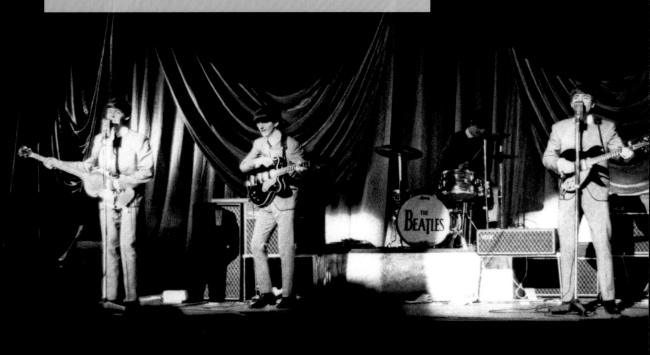

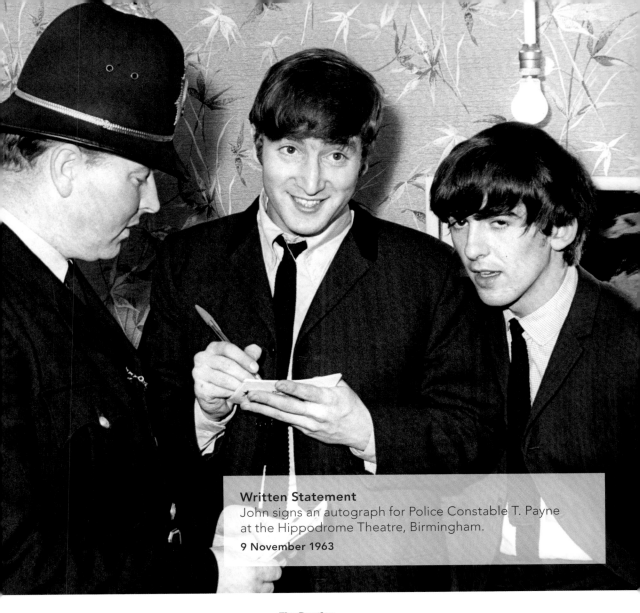

Written Statement
John signs an autograph for Police Constable T. Payne at the Hippodrome Theatre, Birmingham.
9 November 1963

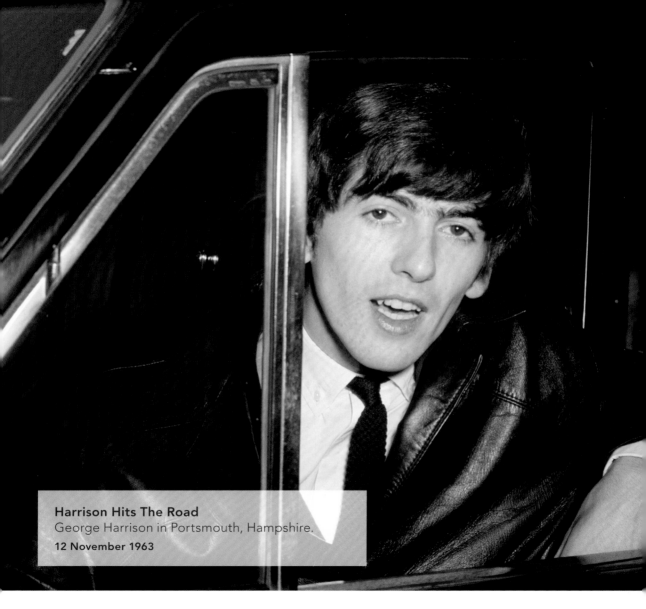

Harrison Hits The Road
George Harrison in Portsmouth, Hampshire.

12 November 1963

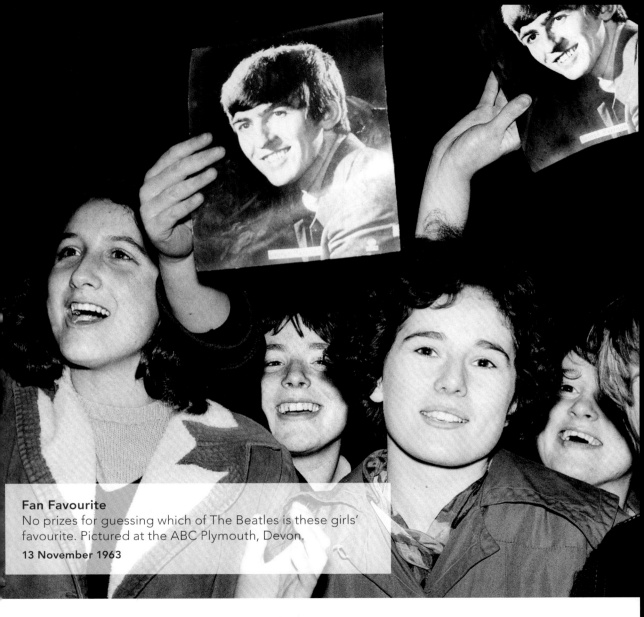

Fan Favourite
No prizes for guessing which of The Beatles is these girls'
favourite. Pictured at the ABC Plymouth, Devon.

13 November 1963

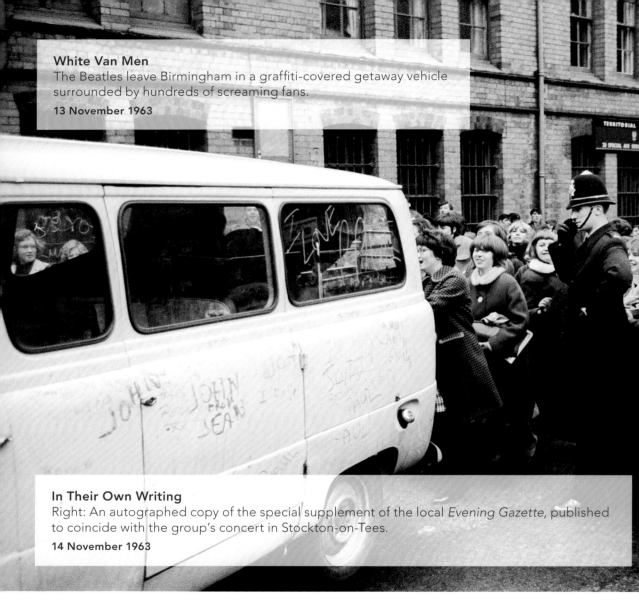

White Van Men
The Beatles leave Birmingham in a graffiti-covered getaway vehicle surrounded by hundreds of screaming fans.

13 November 1963

In Their Own Writing
Right: An autographed copy of the special supplement of the local *Evening Gazette*, published to coincide with the group's concert in Stockton-on-Tees.

14 November 1963

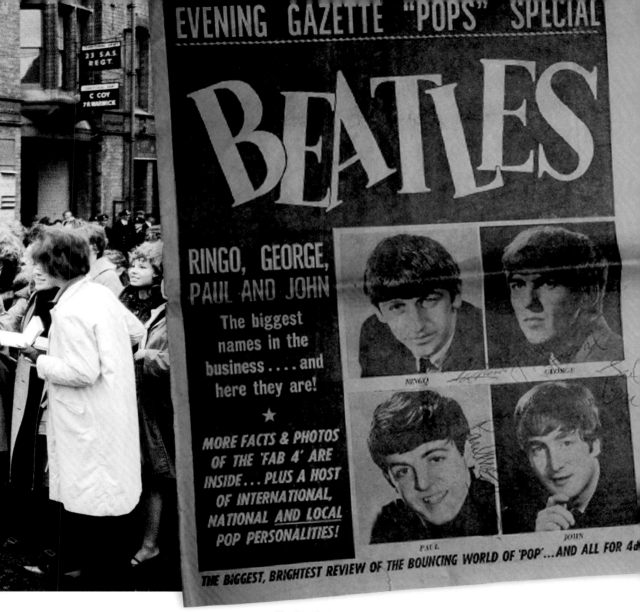

The Beatles

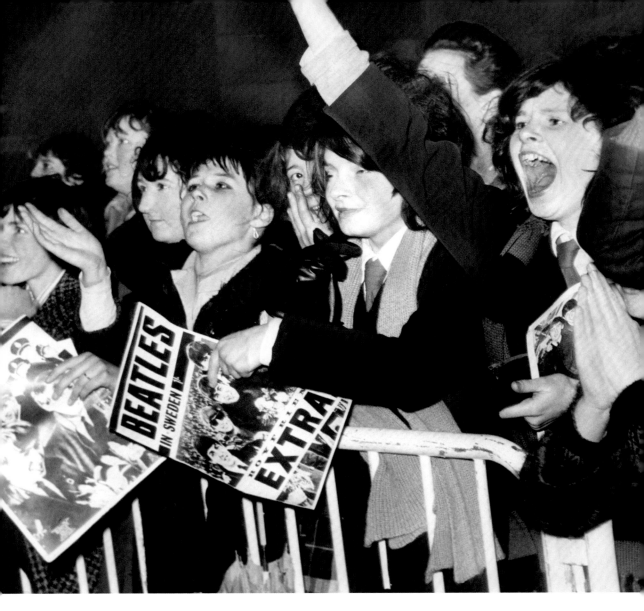

The Beatles

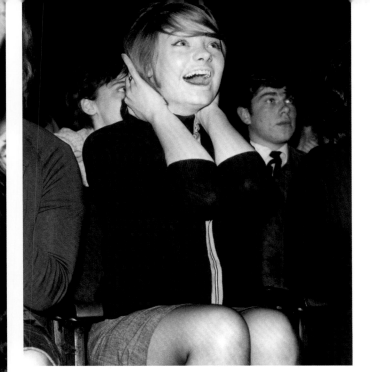

Waiting

Facing page: Another screaming welcome for The Beatles when they visited the Midlands again, this time for two shows at the Gaumont Theatre in Wolverhampton.

19 November 1963

Watching

Top Left: A Beatles fan in ecstasy at the Manchester Apollo.

20 November 1963

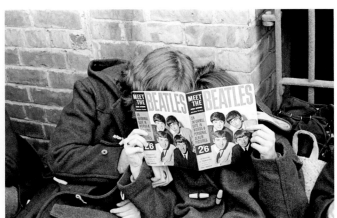

Queuing

Bottom Left: With duffel coats and food supplies in a bag, these Beatles fans queue for tickets in Newcastle Upon Tyne.

21 November 1963

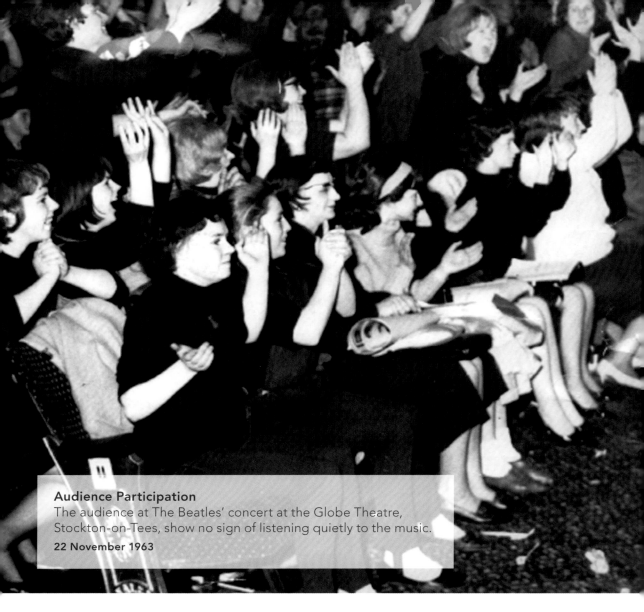

Audience Participation
The audience at The Beatles' concert at the Globe Theatre, Stockton-on-Tees, show no sign of listening quietly to the music.

22 November 1963

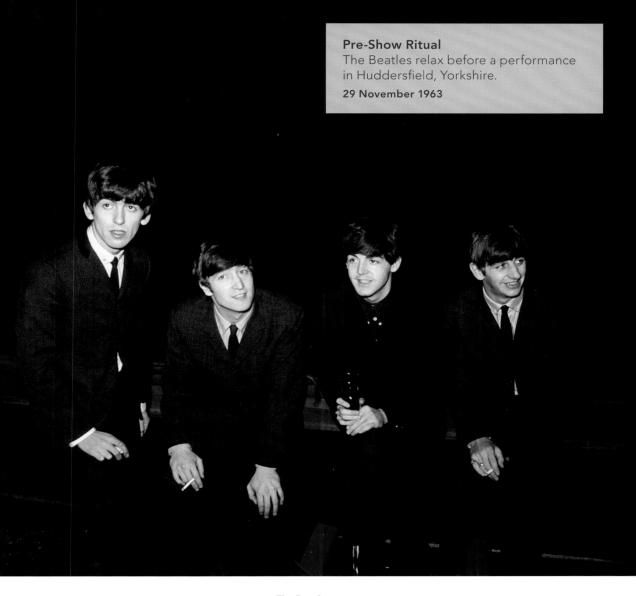

Pre-Show Ritual
The Beatles relax before a performance
in Huddersfield, Yorkshire.
29 November 1963

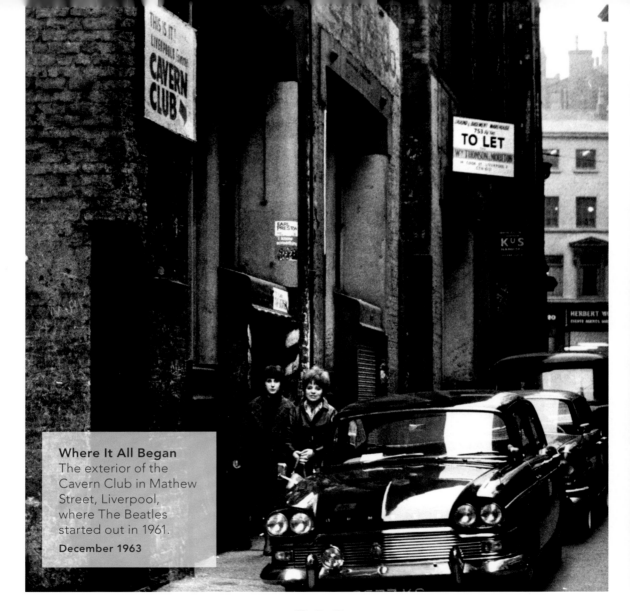

Where It All Began
The exterior of the
Cavern Club in Mathew
Street, Liverpool,
where The Beatles
started out in 1961.

December 1963

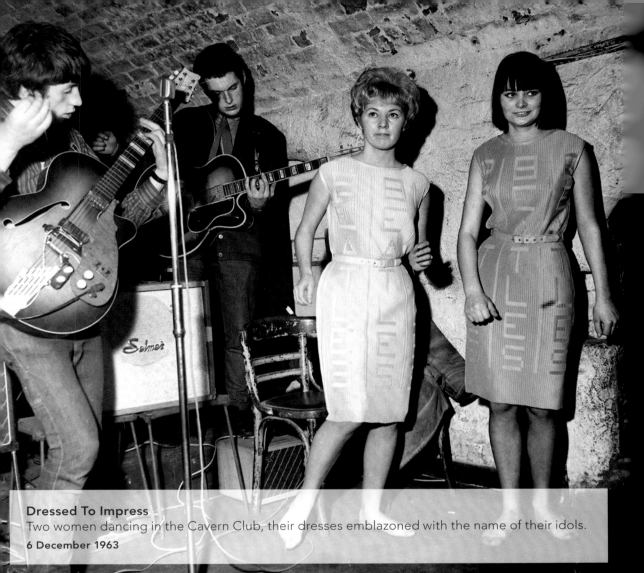

Dressed To Impress
Two women dancing in the Cavern Club, their dresses emblazoned with the name of their idols.
6 December 1963

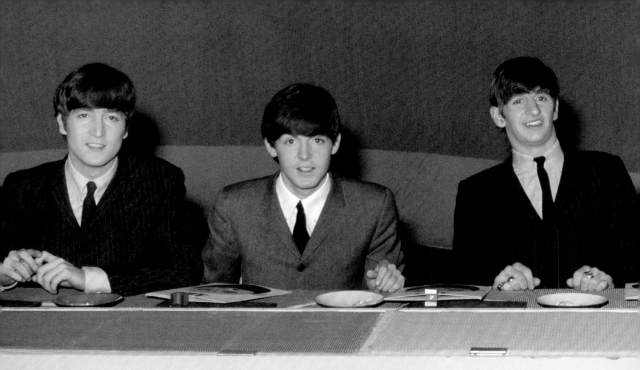

PAUL
McCARTNEY

RINGO
STARR

A Hit Or A Miss?

The Beatles on the BBC TV show *Juke Box Jury*, hosted by David Jacobs. Among the acts whose singles they voted hits were Elvis Presley, The Swinging Blue Jeans and Billy Fury; among those they disliked were old-style crooners Paul Anka and Bobby Vinton.

7 December 1963

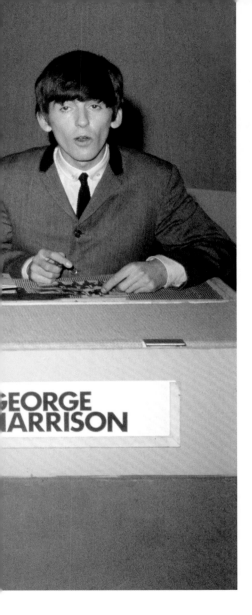

GEORGE
HARRISON

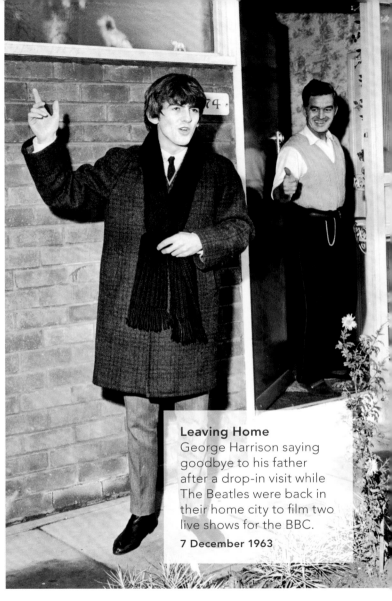

Leaving Home
George Harrison saying
goodbye to his father
after a drop-in visit while
The Beatles were back in
their home city to film two
live shows for the BBC.
7 December 1963

Caught Before The Act

The Beatles stand still for a publicity photograph during rehearsals for a performance on Associated Television (ATV; part of the ITV network) at the station's studios in Aston, Birmingham.

15 December 1963

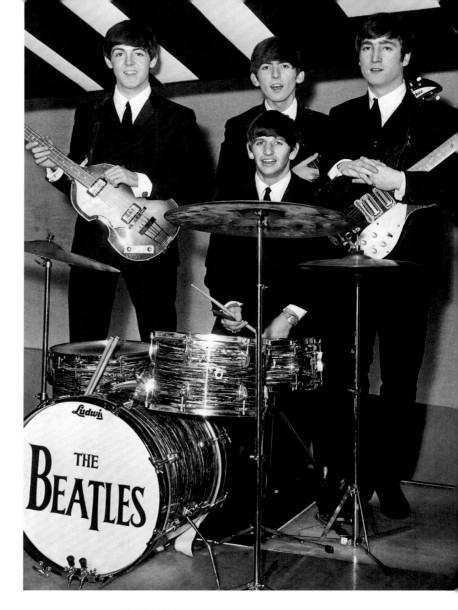

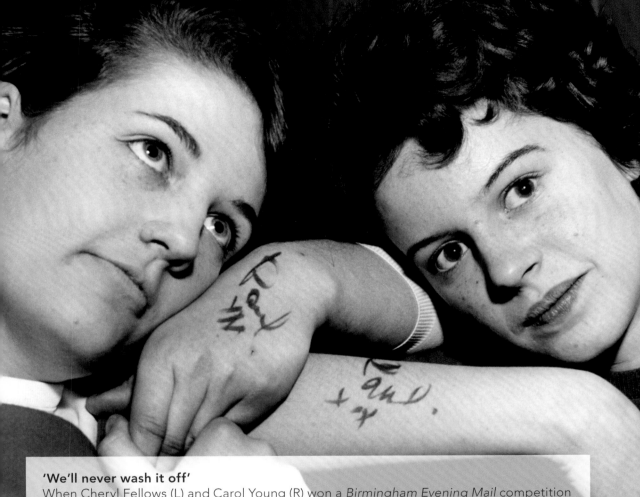

'We'll never wash it off'
When Cheryl Fellows (L) and Carol Young (R) won a *Birmingham Evening Mail* competition – first prize, meeting The Beatles – they got even more than they wished for when Paul McCartney autographed their hands and arms.

15 December 1963

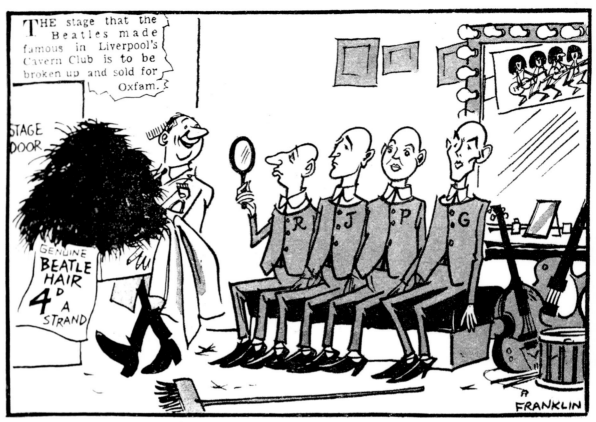

"*Thanks, fellows, it's all for a good cause.*"

'Fourpence a strand'
This was the *Daily Mirror* cartoonist's take on the announcement
that the stage at Liverpool's Cavern Club was to be broken up
and sold, with the profits going to Oxfam.

31 December 1963

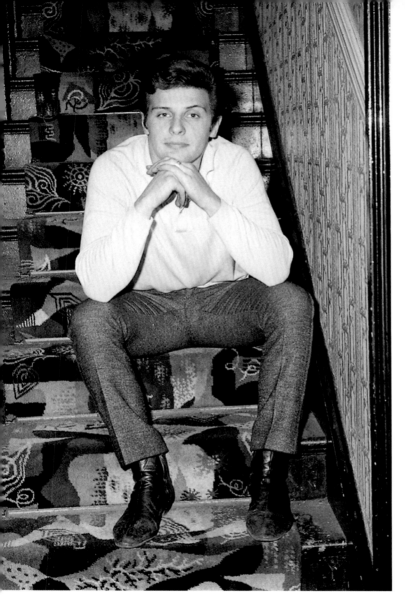

Original Drummer

Pete Best was The Beatles'
original drummer, playing
with them on their first
series of dates in Hamburg,
Germany, and remaining
with them until he was
replaced by Ringo Starr
on 16 August 1962.

1964

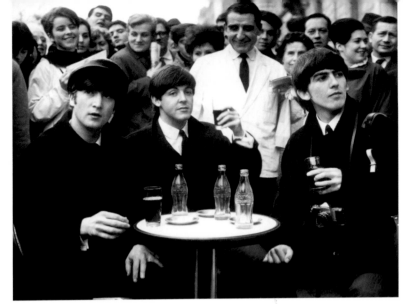

Light Refreshment

John, Paul and George enjoy a glass of the world's most famous soft drink, Coca-Cola, at a street café in Paris while they await the arrival of Ringo, whose flight had been delayed by fog at Liverpool Airport.

14 January 1964

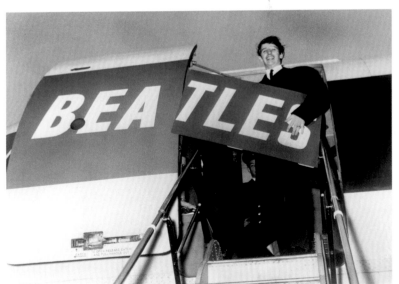

Four-letter Joke

When Ringo Starr landed at Orly Airport the following day he emerged from the plane with a placard identifying the one thing better than British European Airways (BEA).

15 January 1964

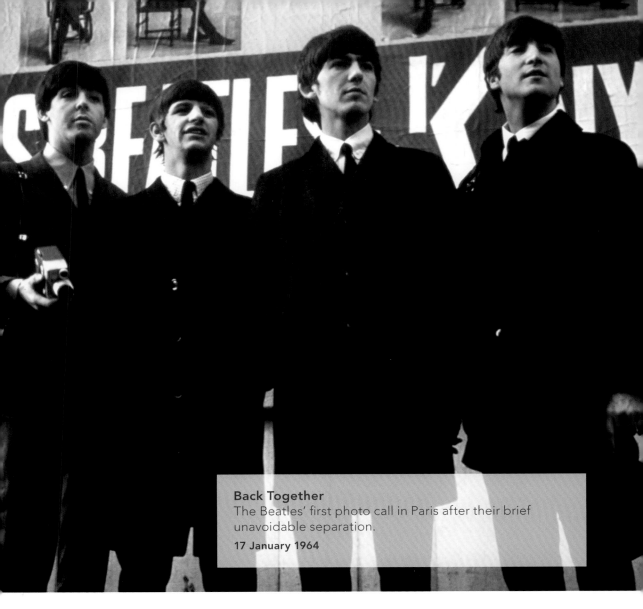

Back Together
The Beatles' first photo call in Paris after their brief unavoidable separation.

17 January 1964

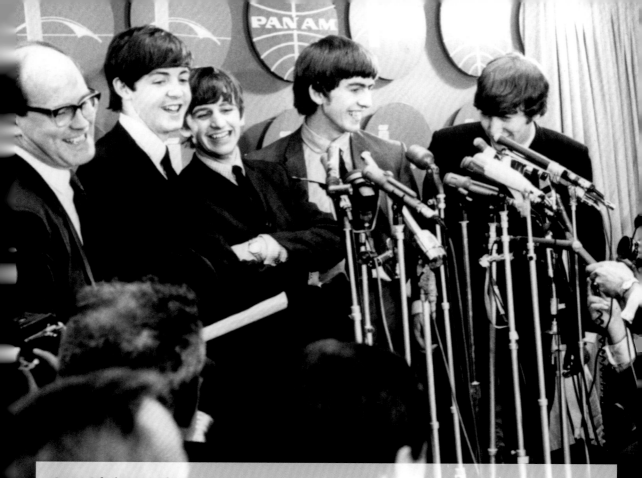

Start Of The British Invasion

The Beatles hold a press conference on their arrival at New York Kennedy Airport, which had recently had its name changed from Idlewild to commemorate the late President Kennedy, who had been assassinated less than two months earlier.

7 February 1964

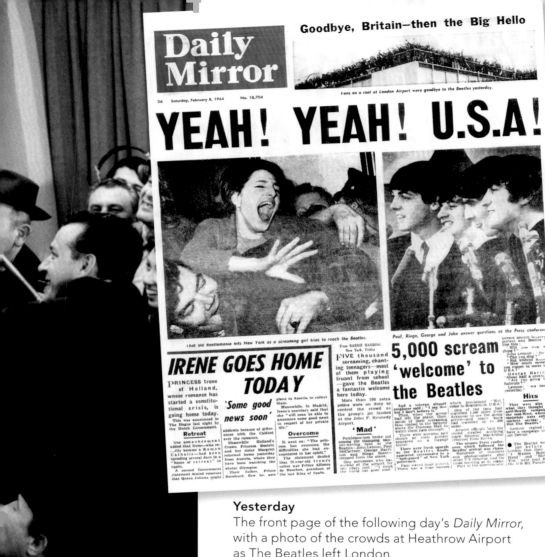

Goodbye, Britain—then the Big Hello

Daily Mirror

3d. Saturday, February 8, 1964   No. 18,704

Fans on a roof at London Airport wave goodbye to the Beatles yesterday.

YEAH! YEAH! U.S.A!

That old Beatlemania hits New York as a screaming girl tries to reach the Beatles.

Paul, Ringo, George and John answer questions at the Press conference.

IRENE GOES HOME TODAY

'Some good news soon'

PRINCESS Irene of Holland, whose romance has started a constitutional crisis, is going home today.

This was announced in The Hague last night by the Dutch Government.

Retreat

The announcement added that Irene—who re-...ly became a Roman Catholic—had been spending several days in a "house of retreat" in Spain.

A second Government statement denied rumours that Queen Juliana might

abdicate because of differences with the Cabinet over the romance.

Meanwhile, in Holland, Crown Princess Beatrix and her sister Margriet returned home yesterday from Austria, where they have been watching the winter Olympics.

Their father, Prince Bernhard, flew his own

plane to Austria to collect them.

Meanwhile, in Madrid, Irene's secretary said that she "will soon be able to announce same good news in respect of her private life."

Overcome

It went on: "The princess has overcome the difficulties she had encountered in her spirit."

The statement denied that 24-year-old Irene's suitor was Prince Alfonso de Bourbon, grandson of the last King of Spain.

From BARRIE HARDING
New York, Friday

FIVE thousand screaming, chanting teenagers—most of them playing truant from school—gave the Beatles a fantastic welcome here today.

More than 100 extra police were on duty to control the crowd as the group's jet landed at the John F. Kennedy Airport.

'Mad'

Pandemonium broke out among the stamping, shouting, waving fans as the Beatles—John Lennon, Paul McCartney, George Harrison and Ringo Starr—stepped from the plane.

A policeman who has worked at the airport for many years said: "I think the world has gone mad."

5,000 scream 'welcome' to the Beatles

And a veteran airport employee said: "I see it—but I don't believe it."

Then, when the group had left the plane, thousands of their screaming fans rushed to the balcony above the Customs Hall to watch them pass through.

There were screams and shouts as their guitars appeared on a luggage trailer.

There were fresh squeals as the Beatles finally appeared, surrounded by a "bodyguard" of New York policemen.

Fans waved huge posters. There was a huge banner

which proclaimed "Welcome to Beatlesville, U.S.A."

One of the fans had travelled 1,500 miles from Arkansas to see the group arrive—and many more had travelled up to 200 miles.

Airport officials said the crowd rivalled anything since General MacArthur returned from Korea.

The airport Press conference which followed the Beatles' arrival was chaos. Hundreds of reporters and photographers, plus seven TV cameras had the room bursting at its seams.

Part of the question-and-

answer session because reporters and Beatles went like this:

"Will you sing something?"

"Can you sing?"

"Not without Ross—How much money do you respect to make in the U.S.A?"

George Harrison: "About half a crown."

"Are you going to get haircuts?"

Lennon: "we had one yesterday."

Hits

They were also asked what they thought of an anti-Beatle campaign in the mid-West, where some motorists were exhibiting stickers saying: "Stamp out The Beatles."

Lennon replied: "We have a campaign to stamp out Detroit."

● The Beatles were told just before leaving London that their records "I Wanna Hold Your Hand" and "She Loves You" were Nos. 1 and 2 in the US Hit Parade.

Yesterday
The front page of the following day's *Daily Mirror*, with a photo of the crowds at Heathrow Airport as The Beatles left London.

8 February 1964

The Beatles
49

Stand By Me
In rehearsal for *The Ed Sullivan Show*, The Beatles' longtime personal assistant Neil Aspinall (C) stands in for George Harrison, who was saving his voice for the live performance.

9 February 1964

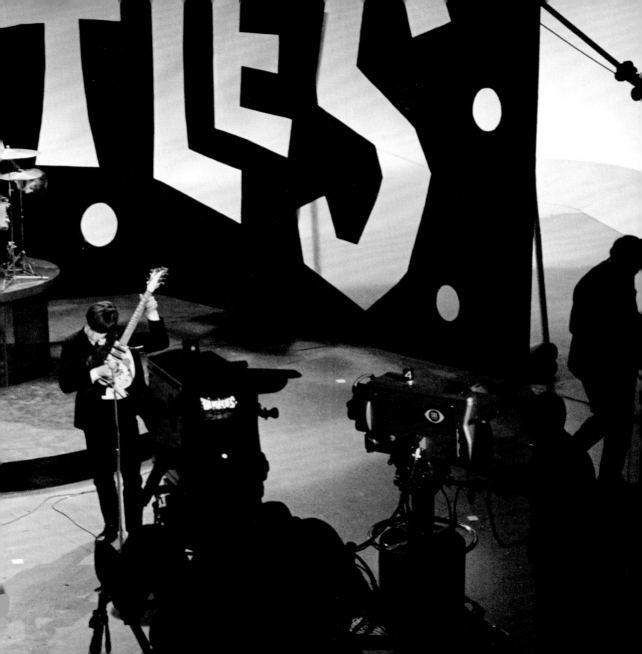

American Admirer
George's throat infection has evidently not been passed to this fan on the streets of New York awaiting a glimpse of The Beatles.

9 February 1964

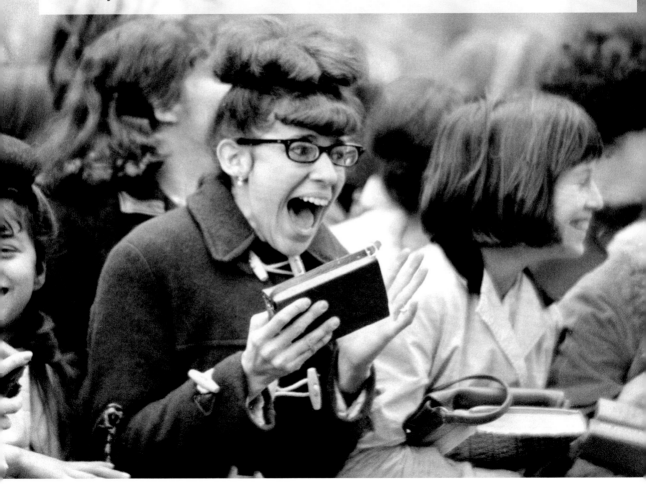

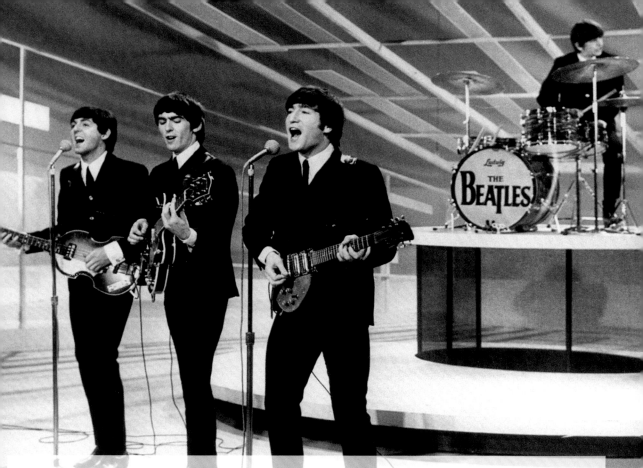

Going Out Across The Nation
The first of The Beatles' three consecutive live Sunday performances on *The Ed Sullivan Show* attracted 73 million viewers. The high point of each show was their current US No. 1, 'I Want To Hold Your Hand'.
9 February 1964

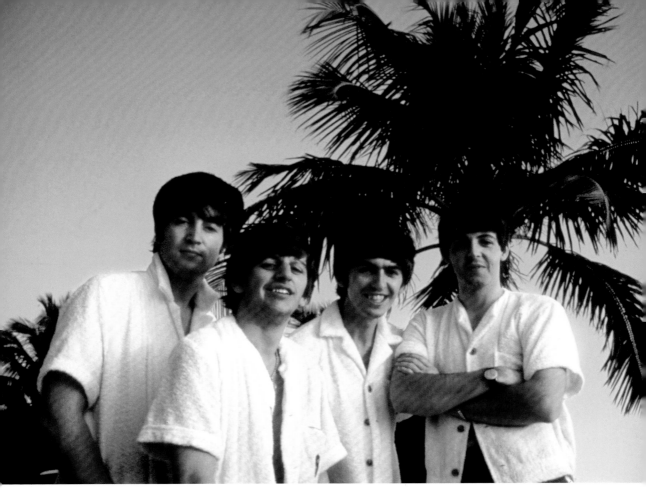

Valentine's Day
The Beatles relax at the Deauville Hotel, Miami Beach, Florida.

14 February 1964

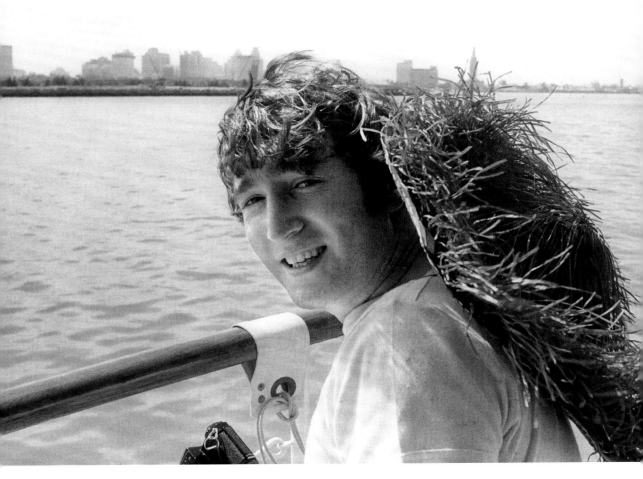

Boat And Boater

John Lennon wearing a grass and straw bonnet in Miami, Florida.

17 February 1964

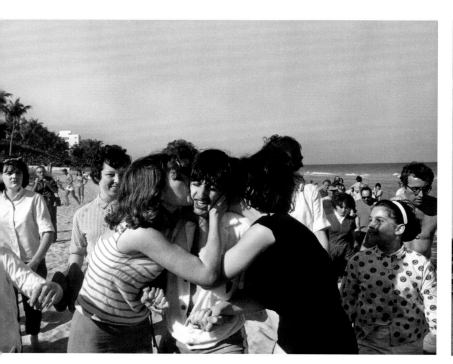

The Cheek Of It
Ringo is grabbed by two
high school girls on the
beach in Miami, Florida.

18 February 1964

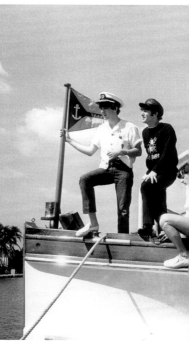

Day Trippers
The Beatles on the deck
of the yacht on which
they made a five-hour trip
around Miami, Florida.

18 February 1964

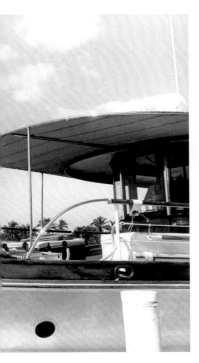
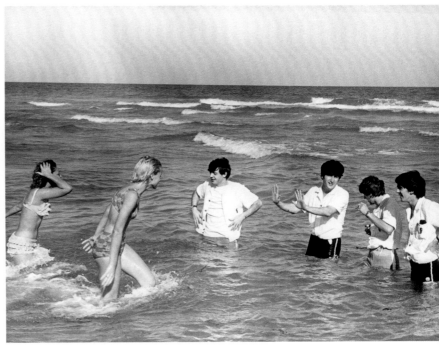

Sea Creatures
The Beatles, still fully clothed, frolic in the sea with a couple of high-school girls off Miami, Florida.

18 February 1964

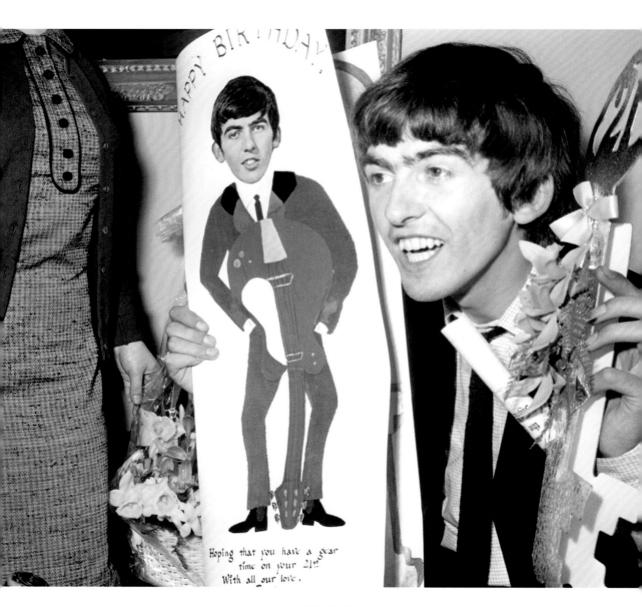

Hoping that you have a gear
time on your 21ˢᵗ
With all our love.

Birthday Boy

Left: George received 52 mail sacks containing around 30,000 birthday cards. Two fans even sent him a door for the thousands of 21st birthday keys he received.

25 February 1964

Model Material

John Lennon holds an effigy that he made of himself. Some people found it a bit disturbing, but it doesn't seem to faze its creator: art is meant to shock.

c.1964

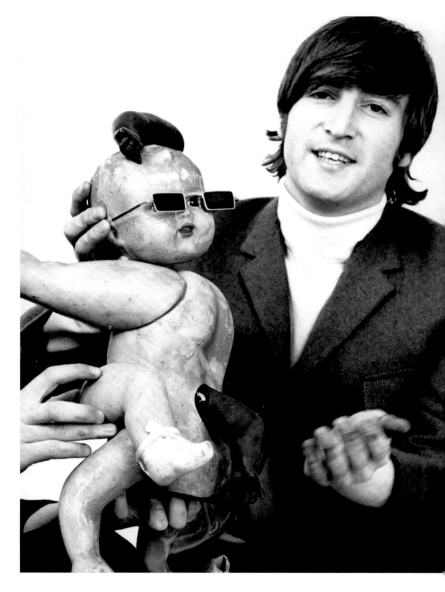

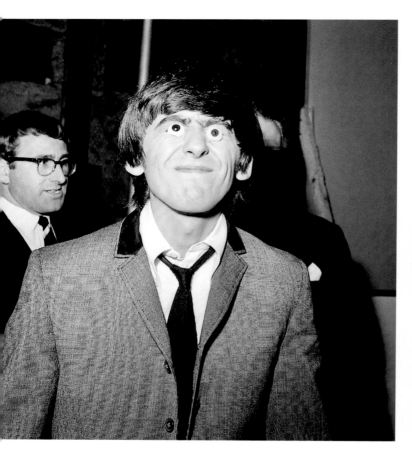

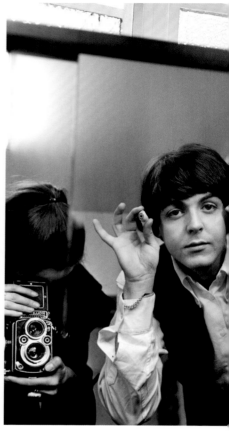

A New Look
George Harrison with glass eyes while The Beatles' details were being taken for Madame Tussaud's during the filming of *A Hard Day's Night* at Twickenham Film Studios.

12 March 1964

Every Little Detail
Paul McCartney holds up his waxwork's eyes so that they can be compared with the real things.

12 March 1964

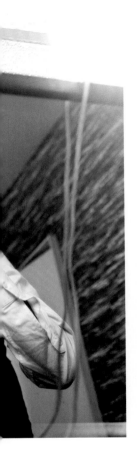
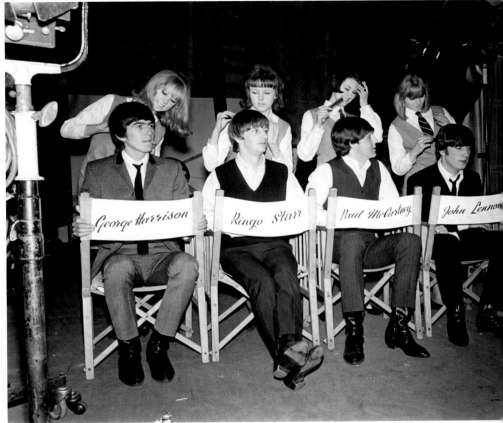

Comb Together

As The Beatles pose for photographs during filming of *A Hard Day's Night* at Madame Tussaud's in London, stylists make sure that none of them has a hair out of place.

12 March 1964

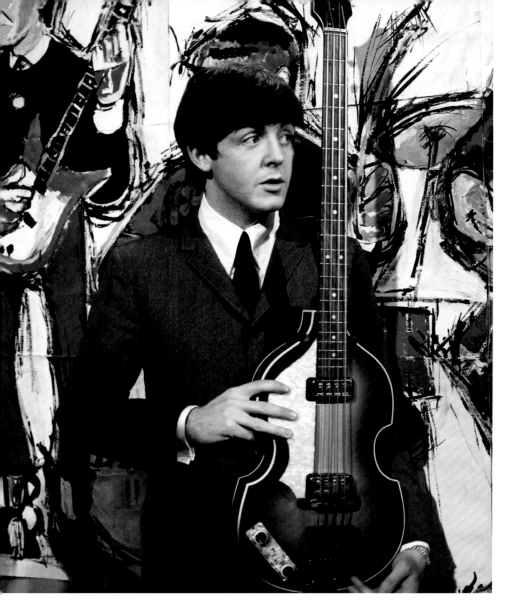
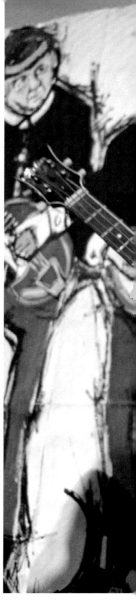

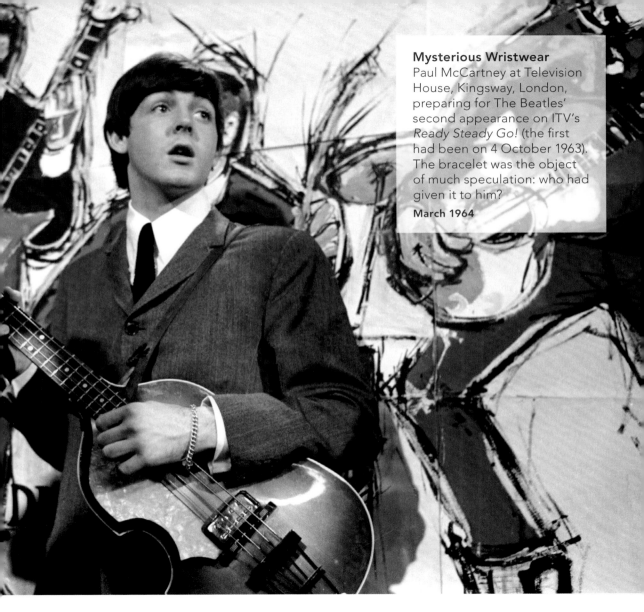

Mysterious Wristwear
Paul McCartney at Television House, Kingsway, London, preparing for The Beatles' second appearance on ITV's *Ready Steady Go!* (the first had been on 4 October 1963). The bracelet was the object of much speculation: who had given it to him?

March 1964

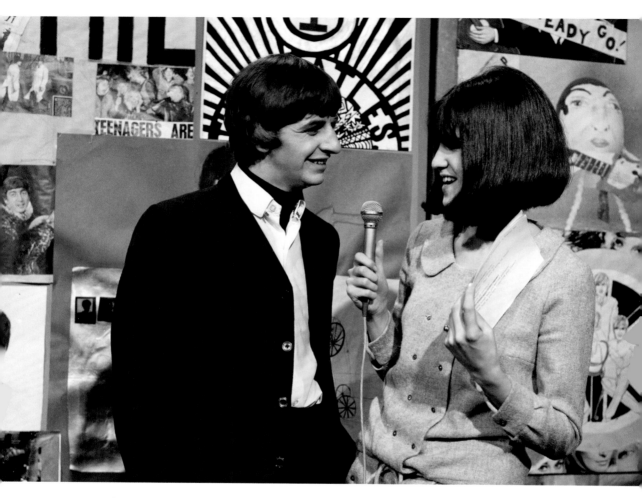

Queen Of The Mods
Ringo Starr interviewed on *Ready Steady Go!* by hostess Cathy McGowan, the fan-turned-compère who, in the view of many, made it cool to be uncool.
20 March 1964

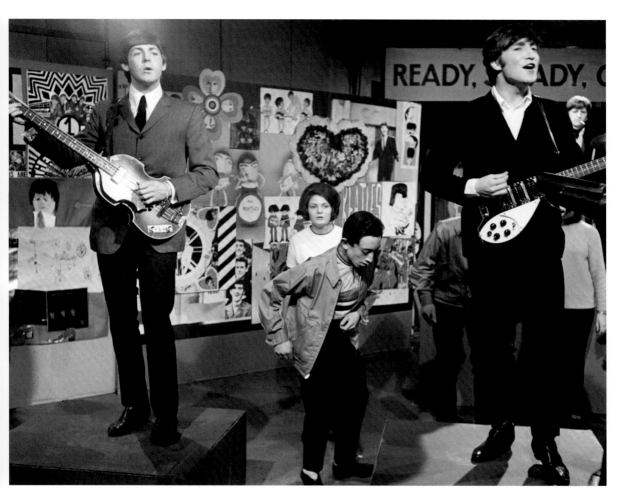

Unplugged

On Ready Steady Go! The Beatles performed 'It Won't Be Long', 'You Can't Do That' and their No. 1 'Can't Buy Me Love'. Note the absence of wiring: that's because they mimed.

20 March 1964

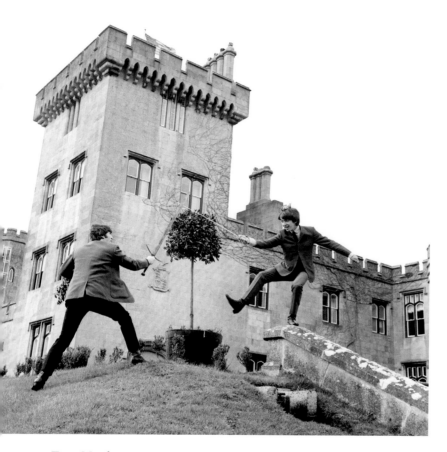

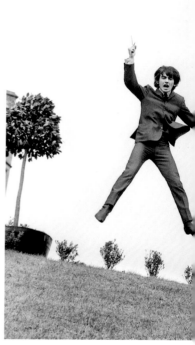

Two Musketeers
John Lennon and George Harrison fool around in the grounds of Dromoland Castle in Ireland, where they went for an Easter holiday.

27 March 1964

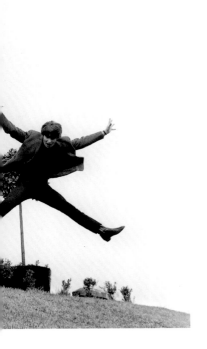

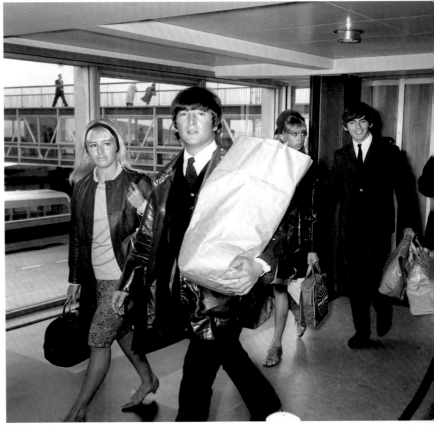

Back To Reality
John Lennon and his wife Cynthia head George Harrison and his girlfriend Patti Boyd through London Heathrow Airport on their return from Dublin.

May 1964

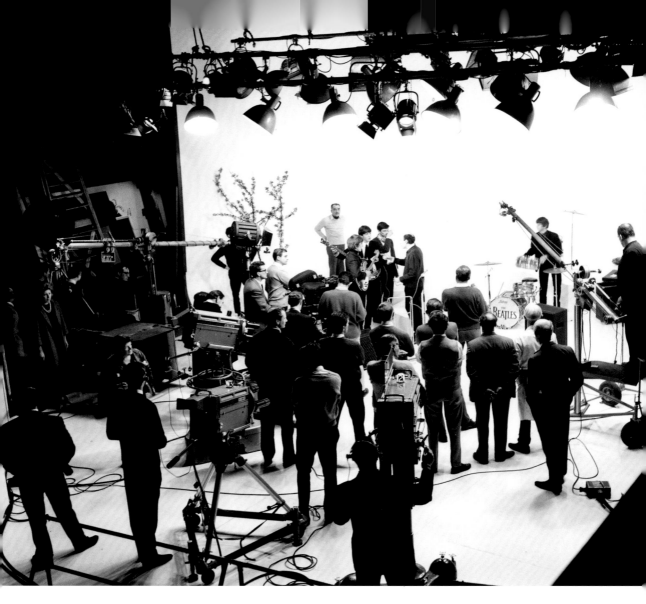

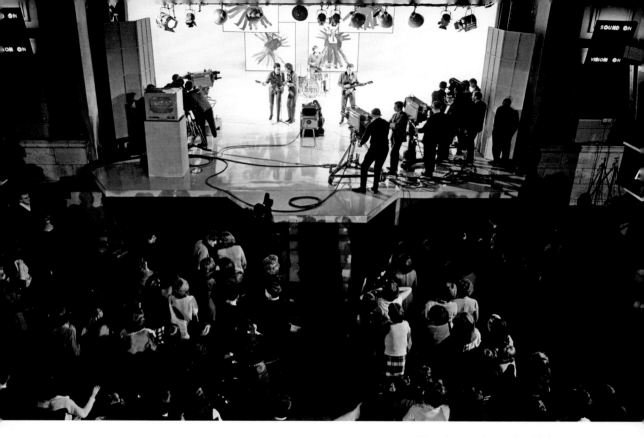

'You know I work all day...'
Still from a BBC TV
documentary about
the making of *A Hard
Day's Night*.
March 1964

That's A Wrap
Left: The Beatles filming the finale of *A Hard Day's Night* at
the Scala Theatre off Tottenham Court Road in London.
31 March 1964

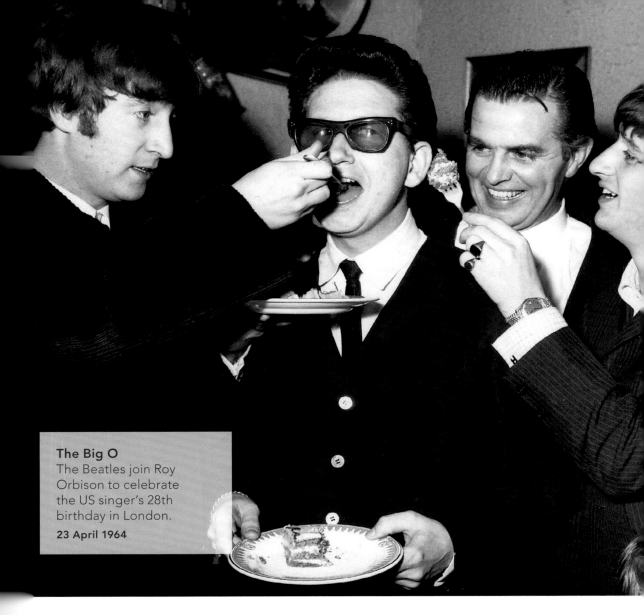

The Big O

The Beatles join Roy Orbison to celebrate the US singer's 28th birthday in London.

23 April 1964

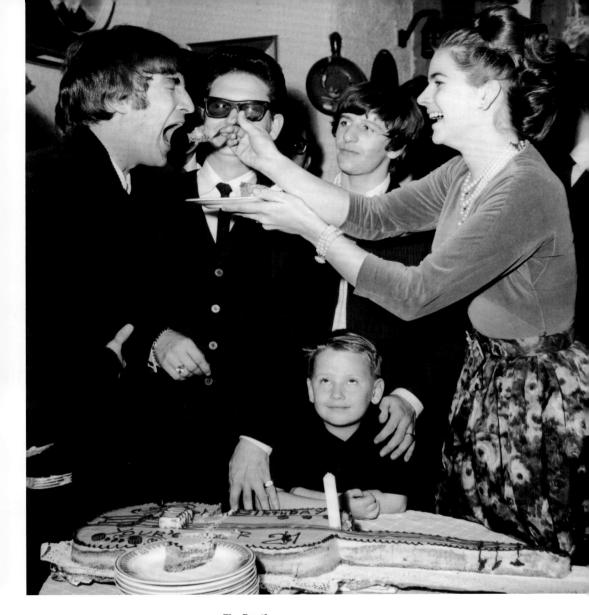

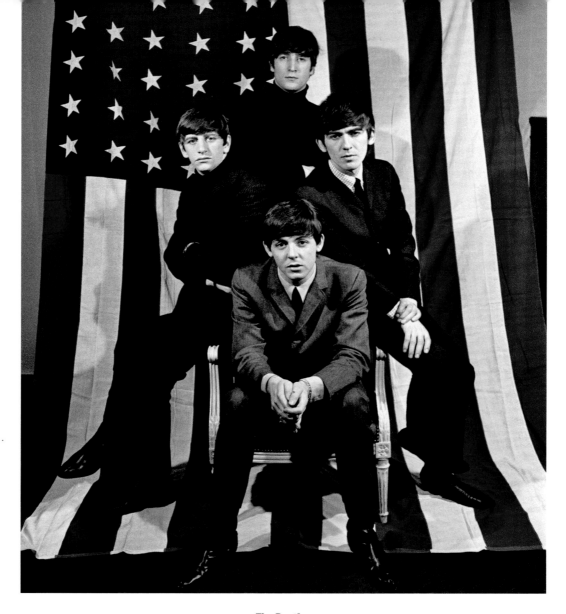

The Beatles

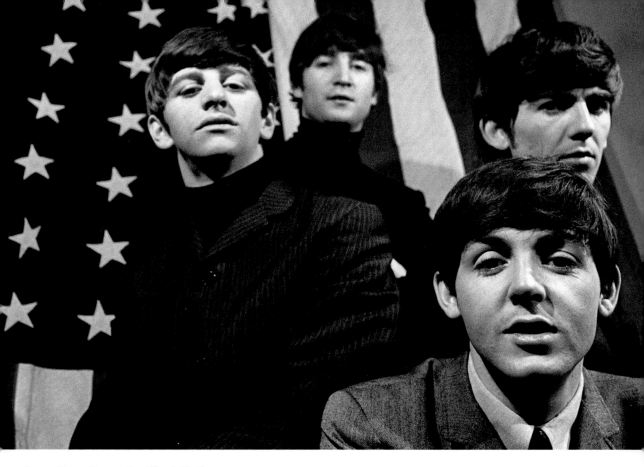

Four New Stars On The US Flag
The Beatles pose for publicity photographs ahead of their
first US tour, a demanding 34-day itinerary with 32 shows in
24 cities, due to commence in August 1964.

April 1964

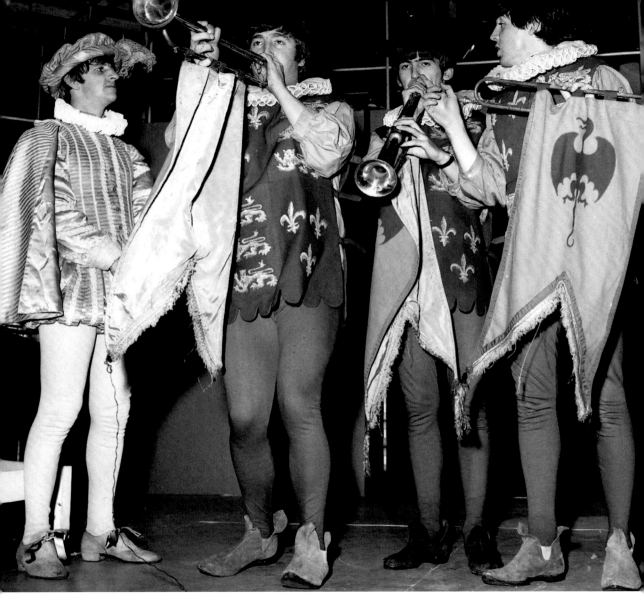

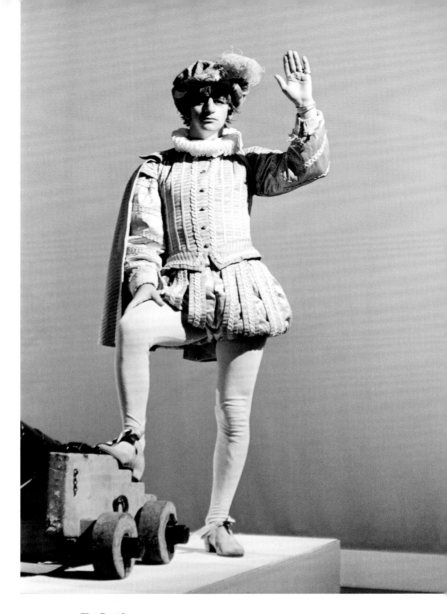

Remaking History
The Beatles in *Around The Beatles*, a TV spectacular recorded at Rediffusion's studios in Wembley, London. While John, George and Paul play heralds, Ringo Starr appears as Sir Francis Drake, firing a cannon at the start of the show.

28 April 1964

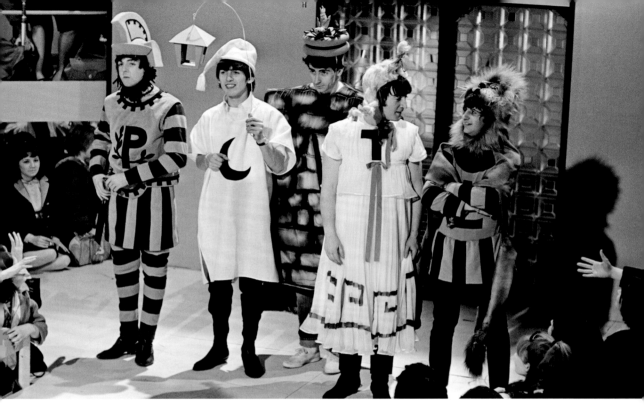

Group Activity

Part of the TV special *Around The Beatles*, filmed at Rediffusion's Wembley Studios, included a spoof of Shakespeare's *A Midsummer Night's Dream* with John (second R) in the female role of Thisbe, love interest to Paul's Pyramus (L), with George (second L) as Moonshine and Ringo (R) as Lion. The group also played a medley of hits and their latest singles. They ended with a version of The Isley Brothers' 'Shout'.

28 April 1964

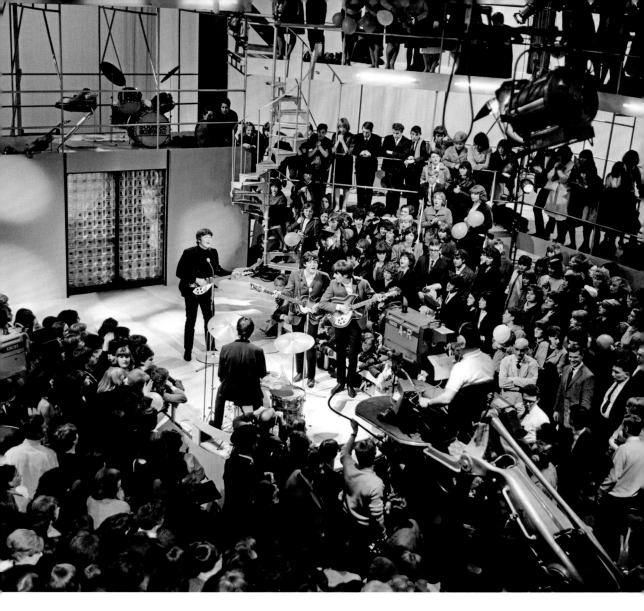

The Beatles

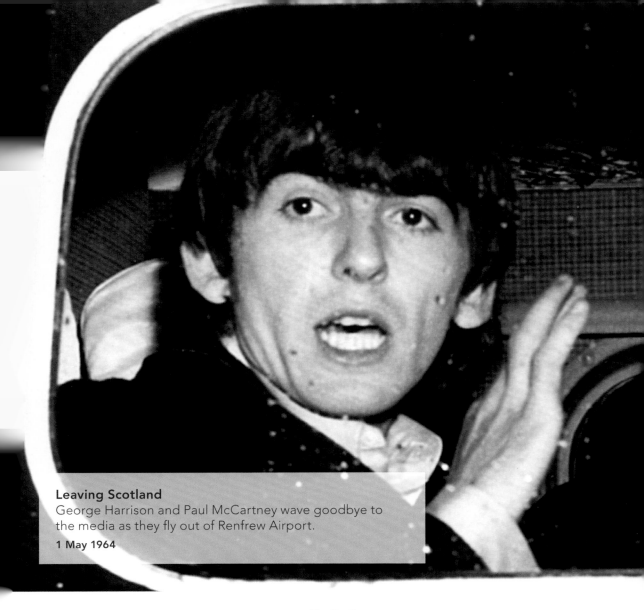

Leaving Scotland
George Harrison and Paul McCartney wave goodbye to the media as they fly out of Renfrew Airport.
1 May 1964

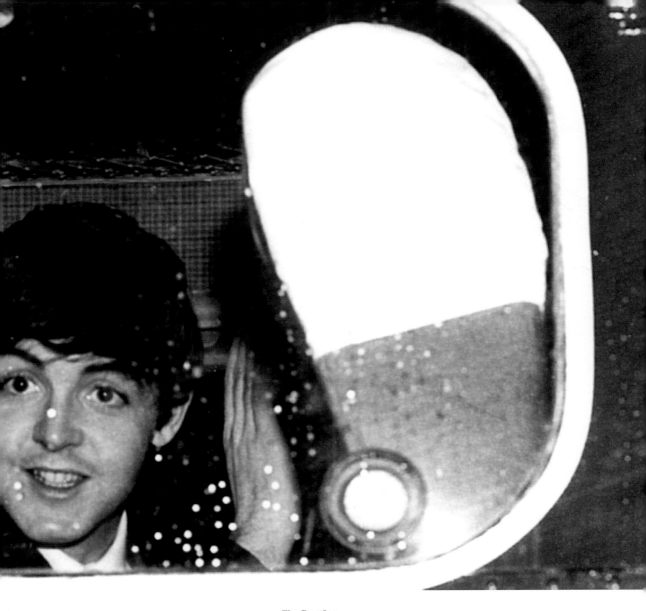

The Beatles

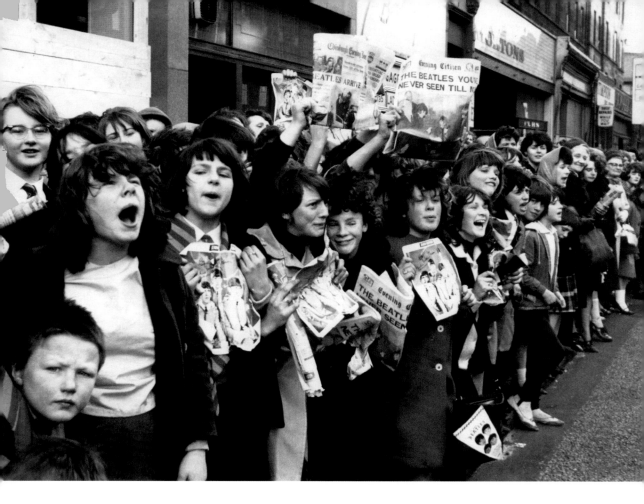

Tartan Army
Fans outside the ABC Cinema in Edinburgh, Scotland,
await The Beatles' arrival ahead of two nights of concerts.

29 April 1964

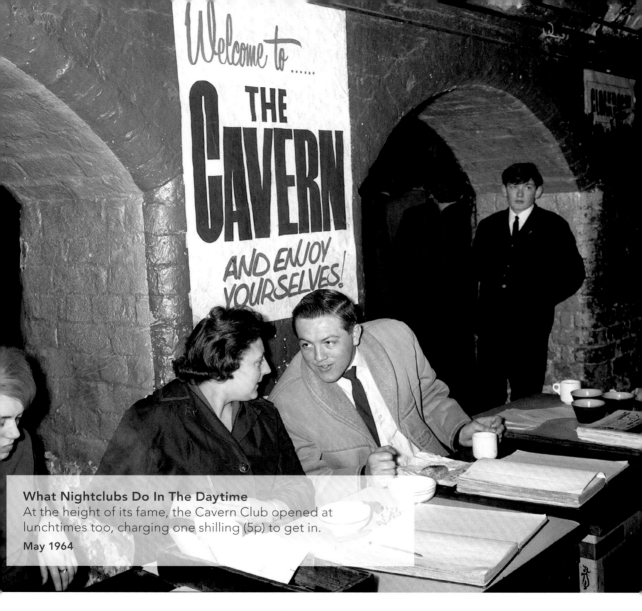

What Nightclubs Do In The Daytime

At the height of its fame, the Cavern Club opened at lunchtimes too, charging one shilling (5p) to get in.

May 1964

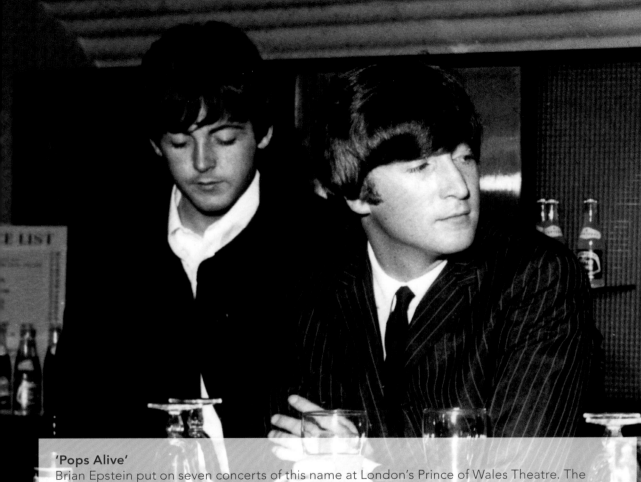

'Pops Alive'

Brian Epstein put on seven concerts of this name at London's Prince of Wales Theatre. The Beatles headlined at two of them, and played 'Can't Buy Me Love', 'All My Loving', 'This Boy', 'Roll Over Beethoven', 'Till There Was You', 'Twist and Shout' and 'Long Tall Sally'. Here the group relax at the bar after their first night at the venue.

31 May 1964

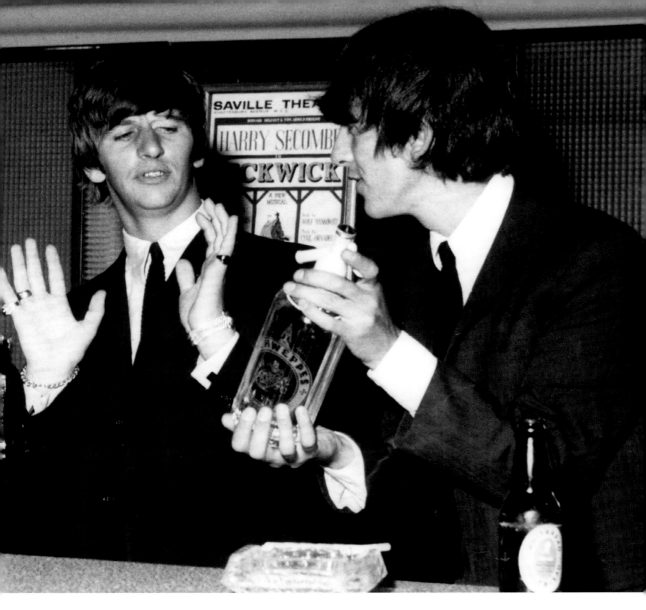

The Beatles
83

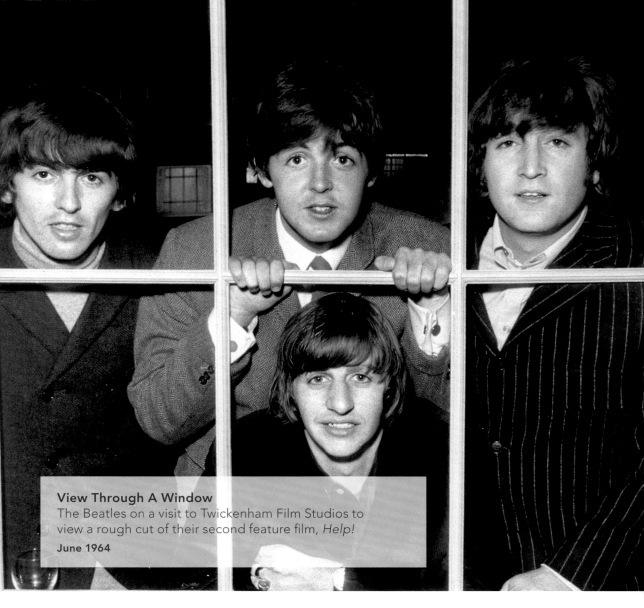

View Through A Window
The Beatles on a visit to Twickenham Film Studios to view a rough cut of their second feature film, *Help!*

June 1964

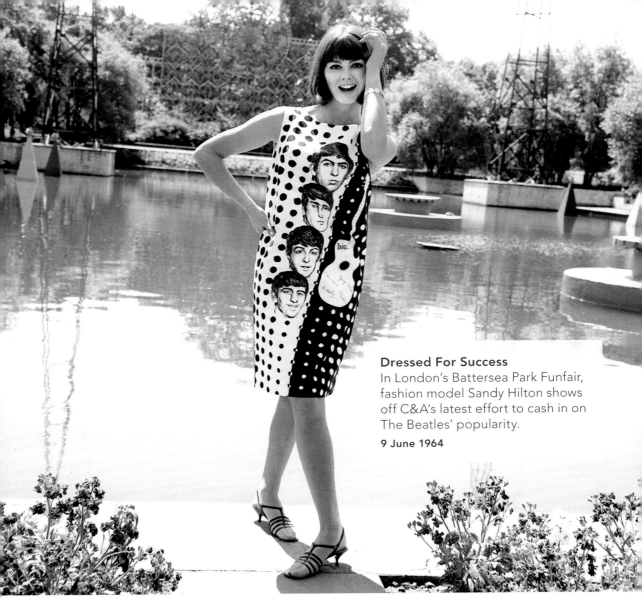

Dressed For Success

In London's Battersea Park Funfair, fashion model Sandy Hilton shows off C&A's latest effort to cash in on The Beatles' popularity.

9 June 1964

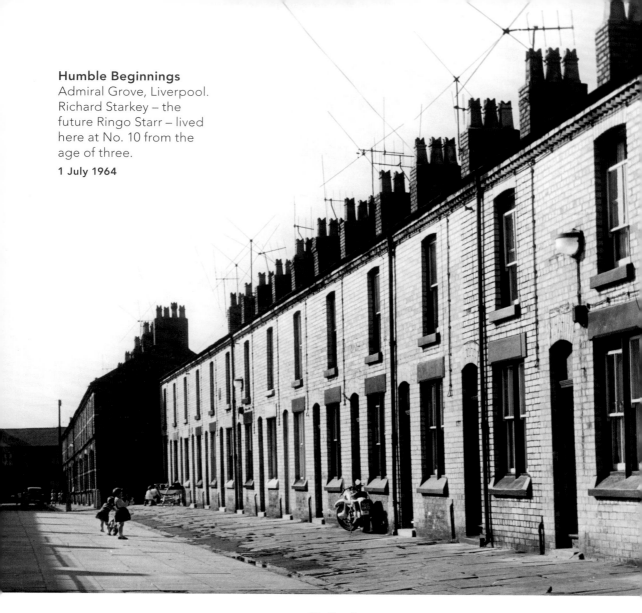

Humble Beginnings
Admiral Grove, Liverpool.
Richard Starkey – the
future Ringo Starr – lived
here at No. 10 from the
age of three.

1 July 1964

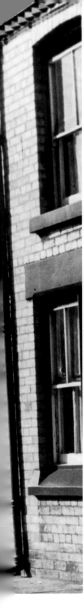
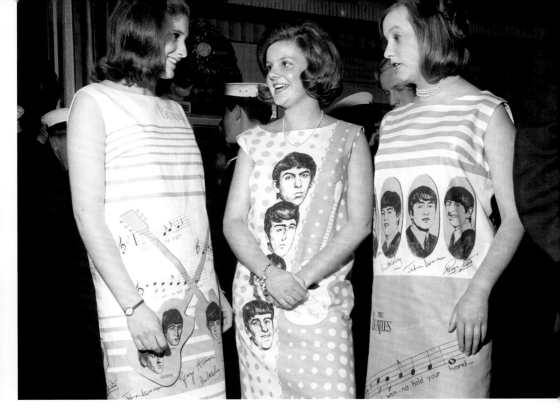

Show Of Allegiance
Fans Jane Cameron, Rosemary Elphinstone and Phillippa Van Steraubenzeezo wear Beatles dresses to the royal charity première of *A Hard Day's Night* at the London Pavilion.

6 July 1964

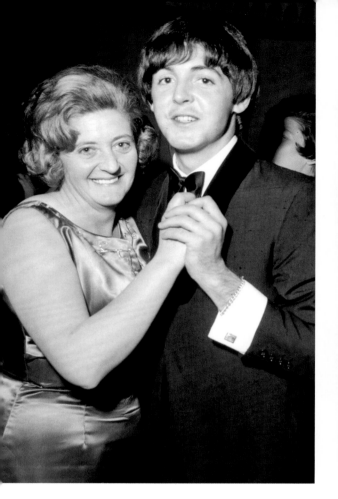

Family Affair
Paul McCartney dances with his Aunt
Joan at an after-show reception at
The Dorchester Hotel in London.

6 July 1964

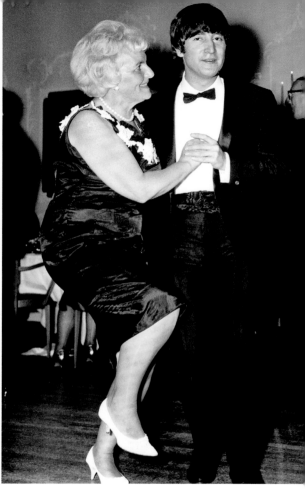

The After Party
John Lennon takes the floor with George
Harrison's mother, Louise.

6 July 1964

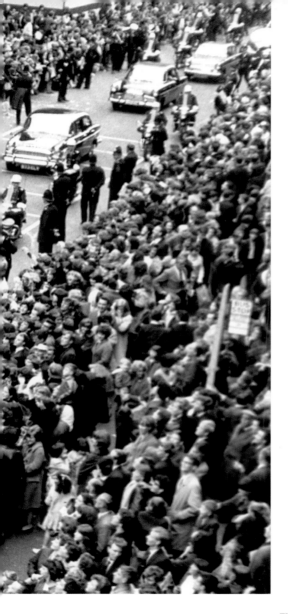

Stately Progress
The Beatles are driven down Castle Street en route to Liverpool Town Hall on the evening of the northern première of *A Hard Day's Night*.

10 July 1964

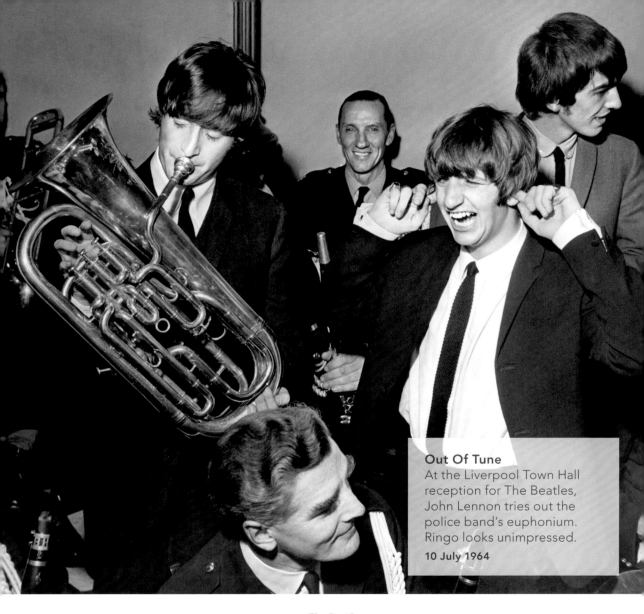

Out Of Tune
At the Liverpool Town Hall reception for The Beatles, John Lennon tries out the police band's euphonium. Ringo looks unimpressed.
10 July 1964

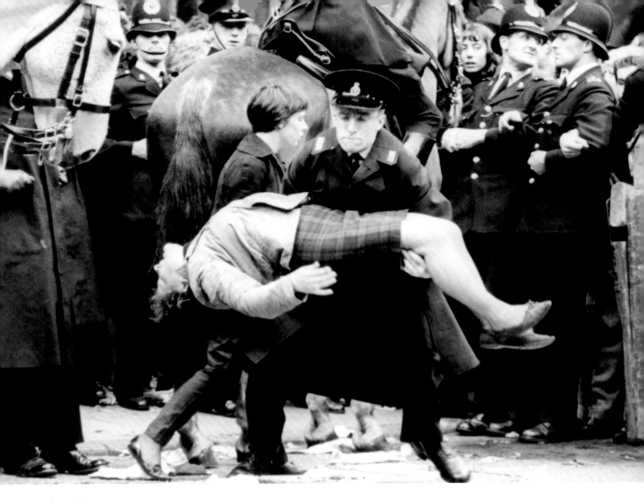

Carried Away

A girl being carried away by an ambulance man after she fainted with excitement at seeing The Beatles outside Liverpool Town Hall.

10 July 1964

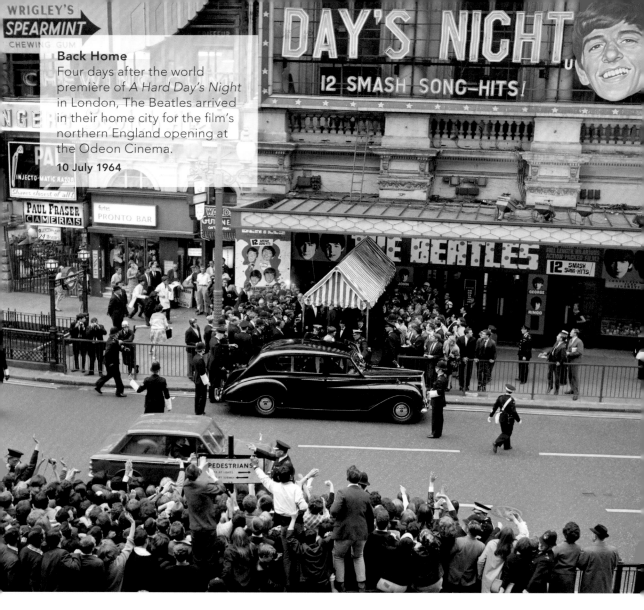

Back Home

Four days after the world première of *A Hard Day's Night* in London, The Beatles arrived in their home city for the film's northern England opening at the Odeon Cinema.

10 July 1964

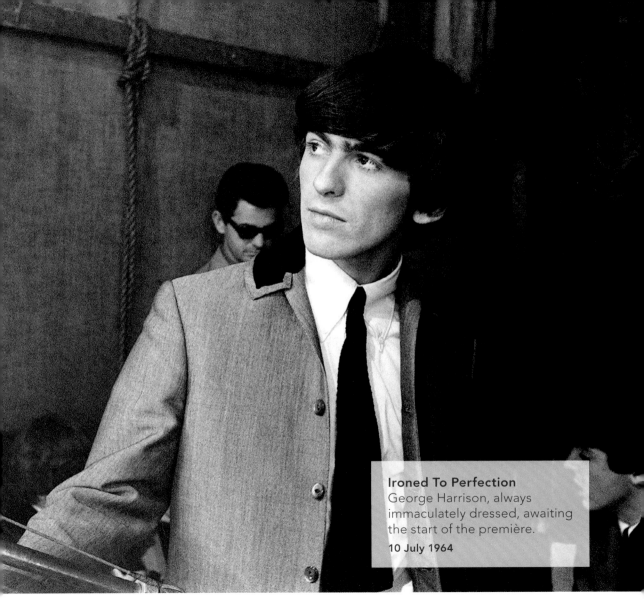

Ironed To Perfection
George Harrison, always immaculately dressed, awaiting the start of the première.

10 July 1964

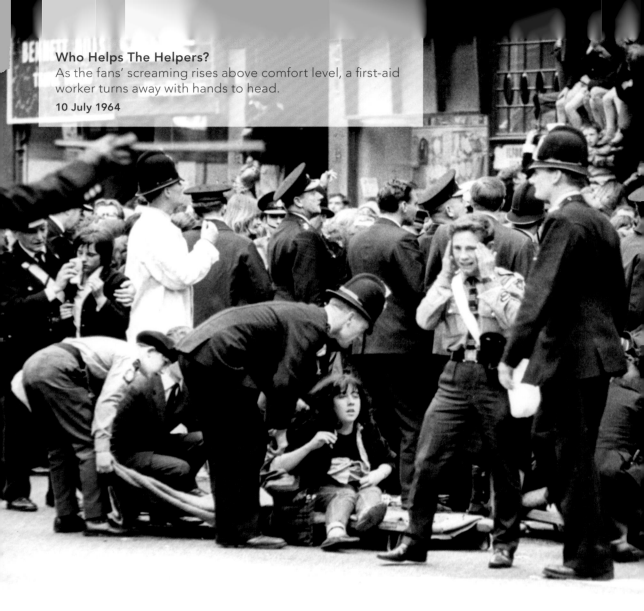

Who Helps The Helpers?

As the fans' screaming rises above comfort level, a first-aid worker turns away with hands to head.

10 July 1964

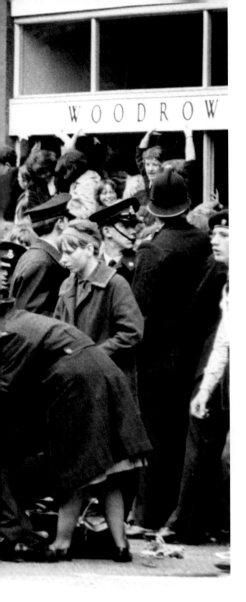

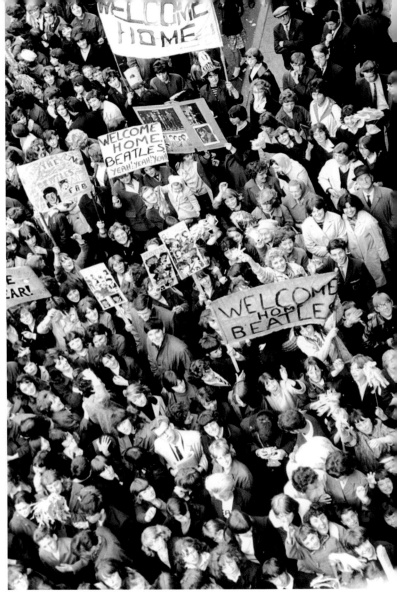

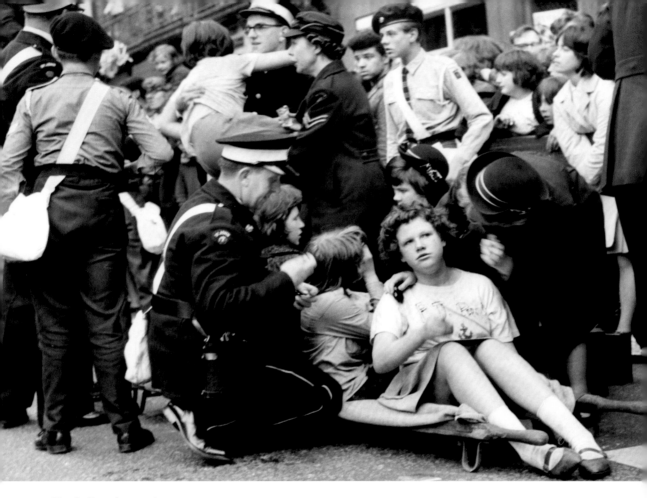

Peak Beatlemania
For Liverpool police and ambulance workers, *A Hard Day's Night* had turned into a pretty tough assignment.
10 July 1964

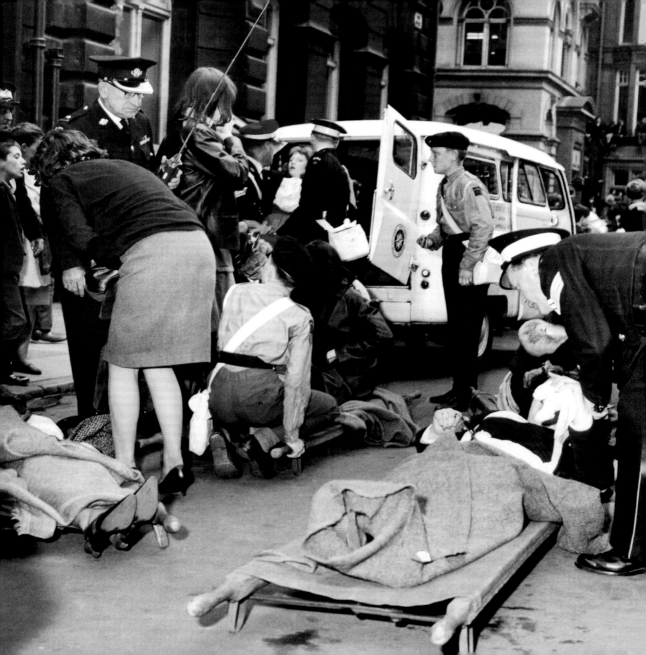

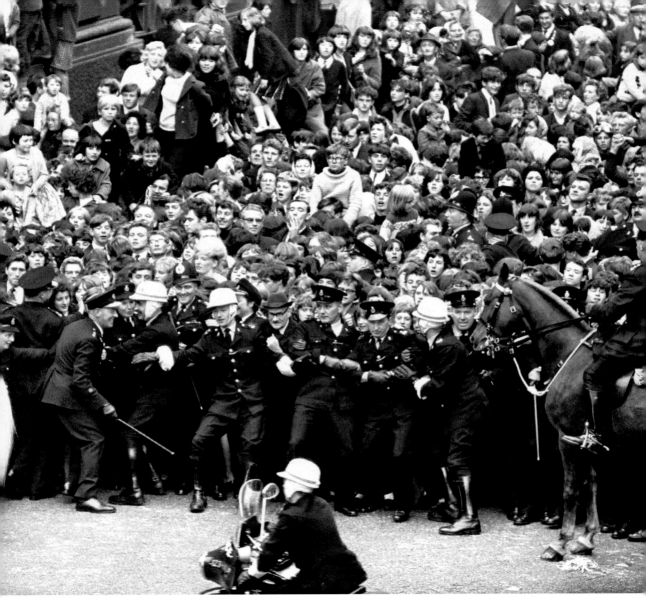

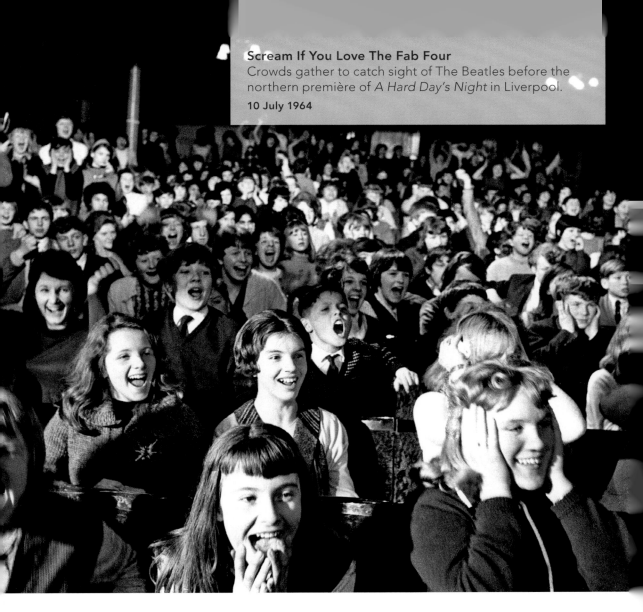

Scream If You Love The Fab Four
Crowds gather to catch sight of The Beatles before the northern première of *A Hard Day's Night* in Liverpool.
10 July 1964

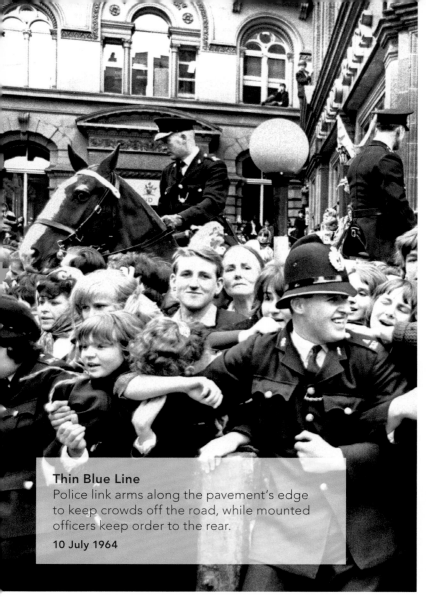

Thin Blue Line

Police link arms along the pavement's edge to keep crowds off the road, while mounted officers keep order to the rear.

10 July 1964

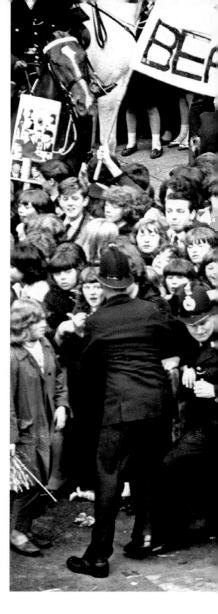

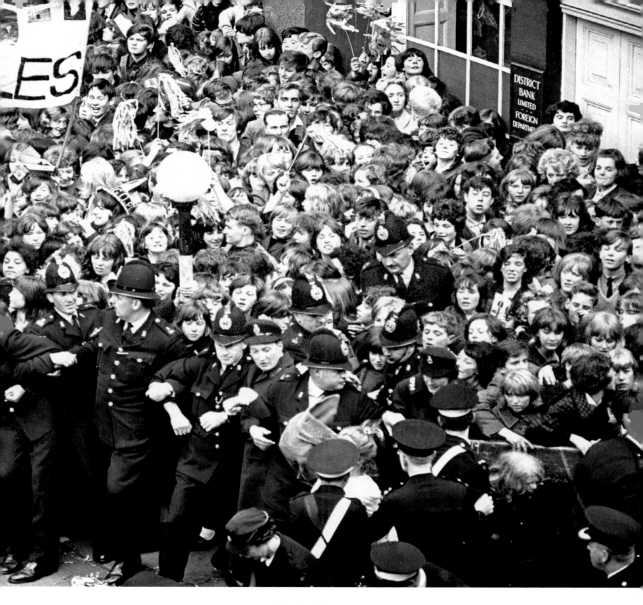

The Beatles

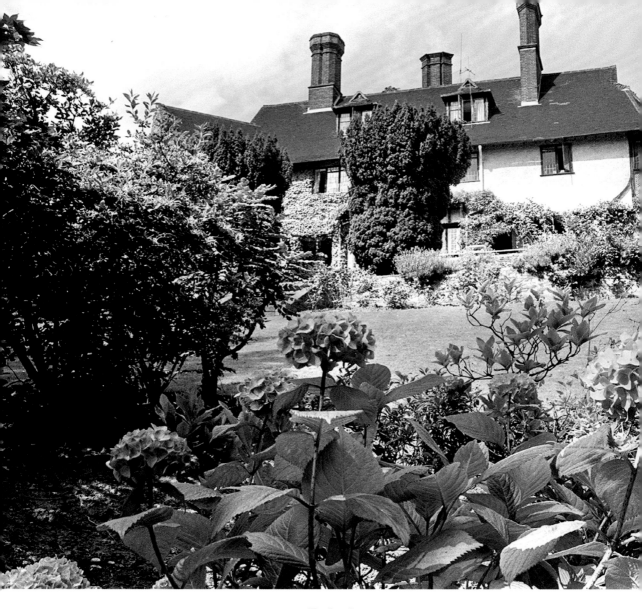

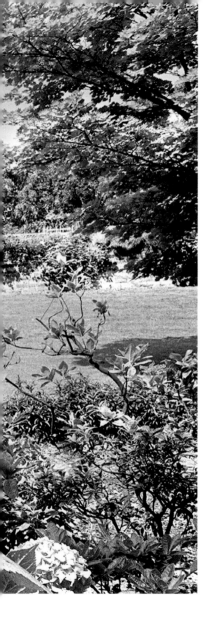

Tudor Revival

Two days after this photograph was taken, John Lennon became the second landed Beatle when he completed the purchase of Kenwood, a mock Tudor mansion in St George's Hill, Weybridge, Surrey.

13 July 1964

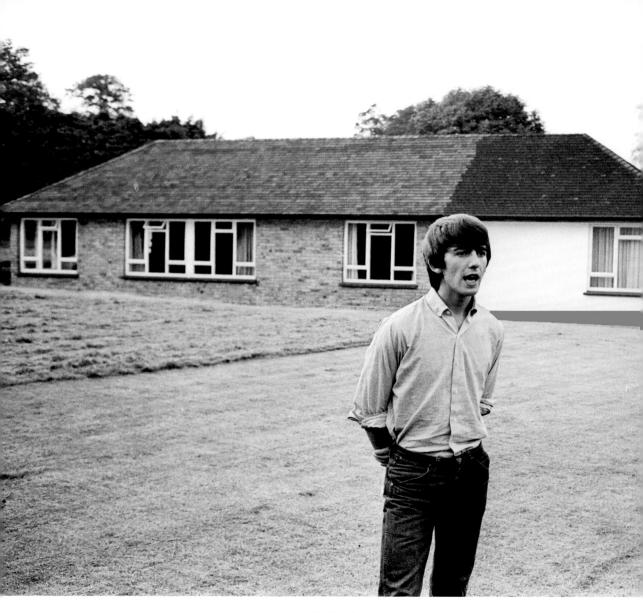

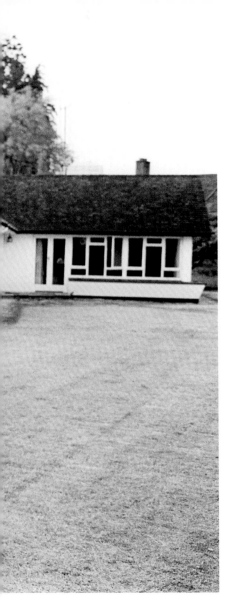

On The Housing Ladder

The Beatles' accountant advised them to invest in property, so George Harrison bought the first house he looked at, Kinfauns, a bungalow on the Claremont Estate in Esher, Surrey.

17 July 1964

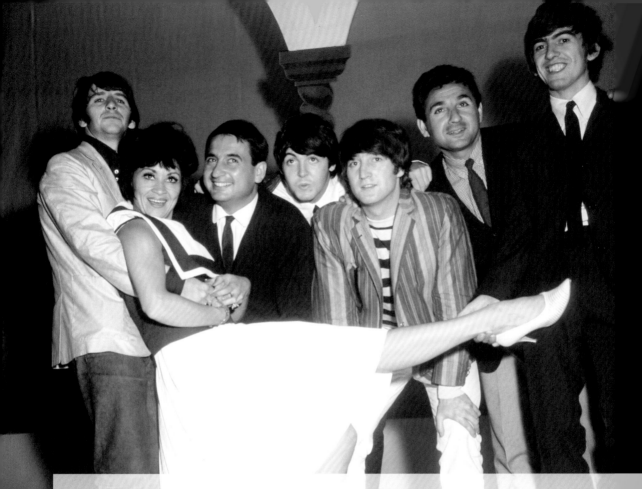

'Blackpool Night Out'
The Beatles starred in a summer show of this name, which also featured American singer and dancer Chita Rivera and British comic double act Mike and Bernie Winters (respectively second R and third L).

19 July 1964

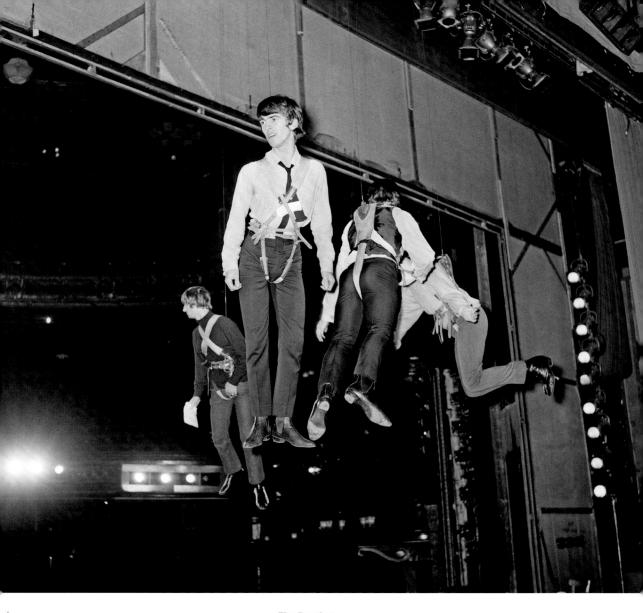

The Beatles
115

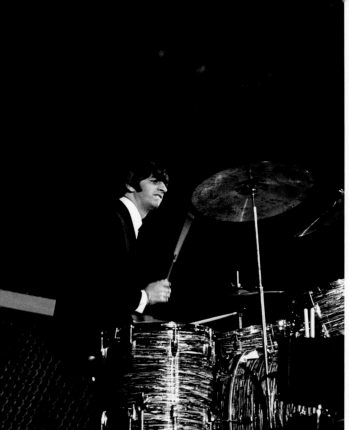
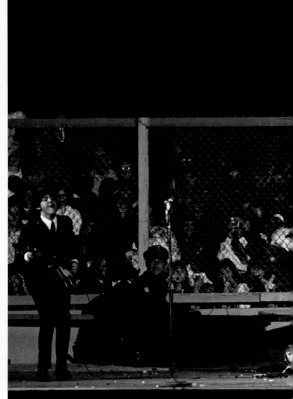

Rocking Las Vegas

Having played in San Francisco on the evening of 19 August, The Beatles flew to Las Vegas, where they landed at 1.30am and were driven to the Sahara Hotel. At 2.30pm they went to the city's Convention Center, did a quick sound check, and then launched into the first of two concerts, one at 4pm the other at 9pm. They were paid $30,000 for the two gigs, but barred from going on to the casinos afterwards because police feared they might be followed by young fans who were too young to gamble.

20 August 1964

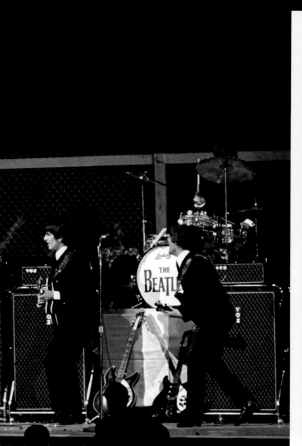
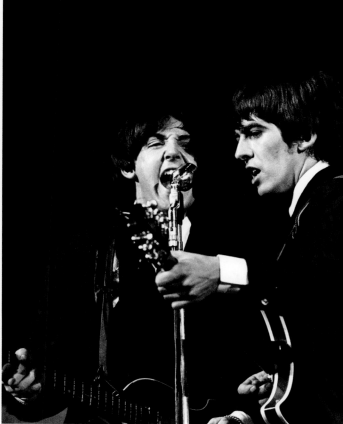

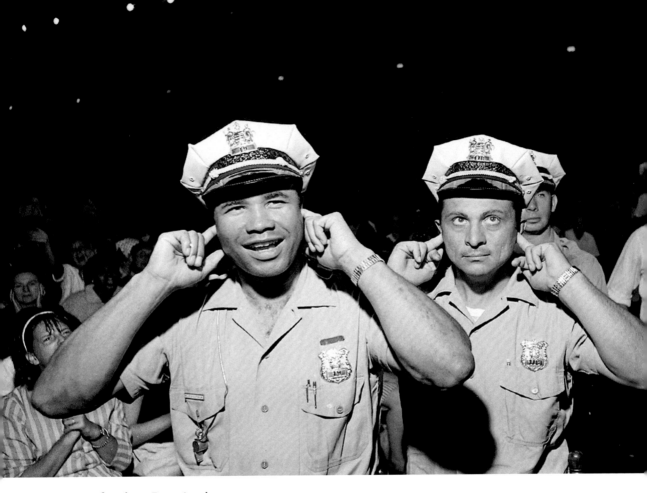

Ear Defenders Required

Two policemen cover their ears at a Beatles' concert during the US tour. Whether the officers are objecting to the band's music or the noise of their fans is a moot point – this syndicated photograph originally got captioned both ways.

August 1964

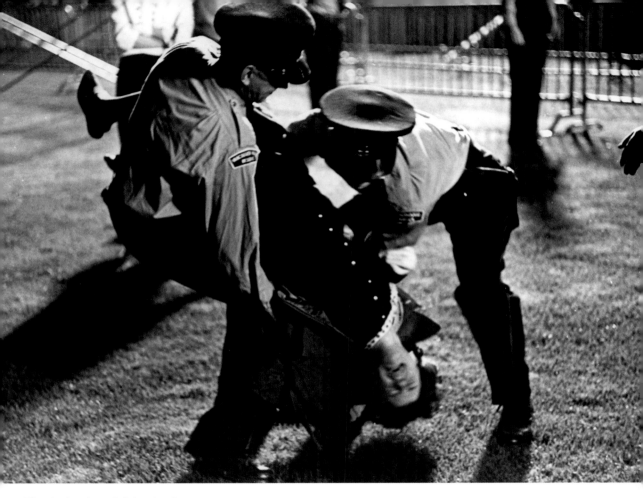

The Imitation Of An Action
Having watched British and US Beatlemania, Canadians were keen not to be outdone, so this was not the only swooning girl the RCMP had to carry out from the group's concert in Vancouver, British Columbia.

22 August 1964

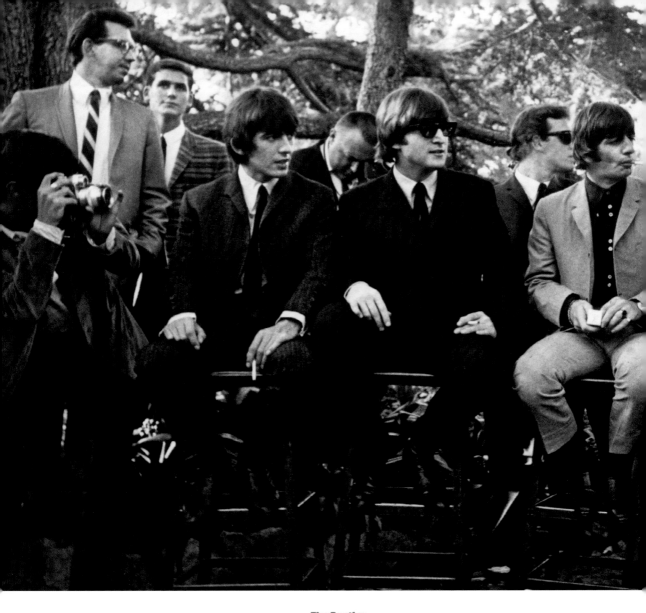

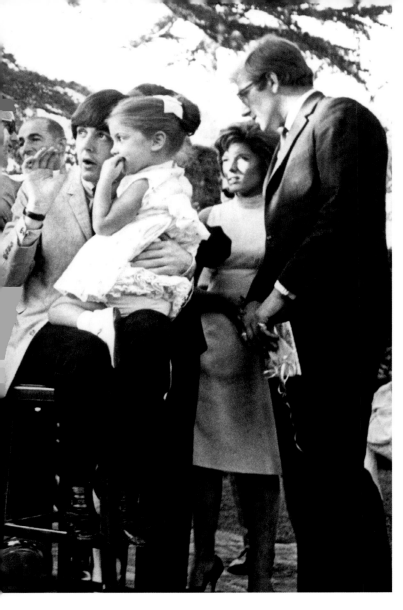

What Does Your Daddy Do?

Paul McCartney holds Rebel Lee Robinson (daughter of Hollywood star Edward G. Robinson) at a reception organized by the Haemophilia Foundation of Southern California at the Livingston Garden, Los Angeles, California.

24 August 1964

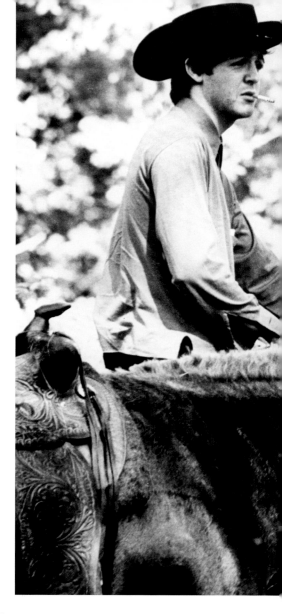

Horseplay

In Los Angeles to play the Hollywood Bowl, The Beatles stay in a rented house in exclusive Bel Air and take advantage of a rare gap in their breakneck schedule to visit a ranch and act like cowboys.

24 August 1964

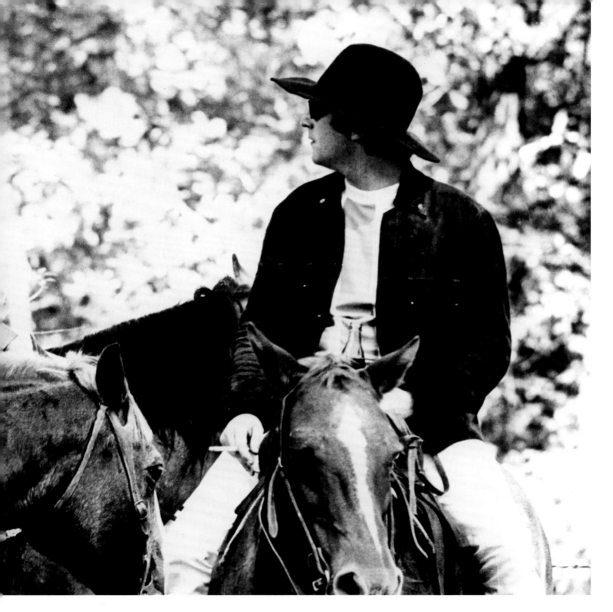

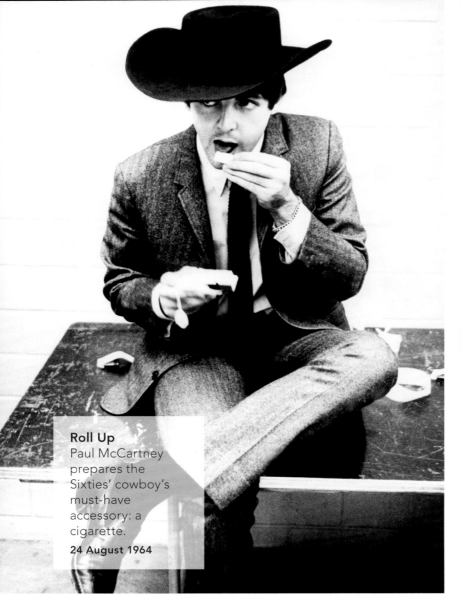
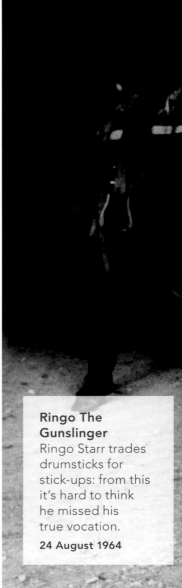

Roll Up
Paul McCartney prepares the Sixties' cowboy's must-have accessory: a cigarette.
24 August 1964

Ringo The Gunslinger
Ringo Starr trades drumsticks for stick-ups: from this it's hard to think he missed his true vocation.
24 August 1964

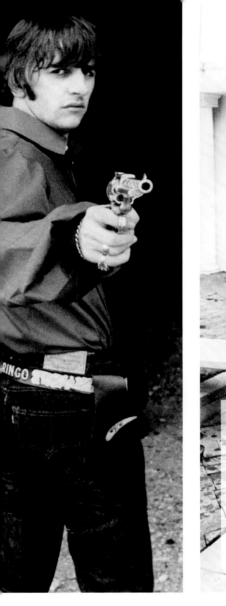

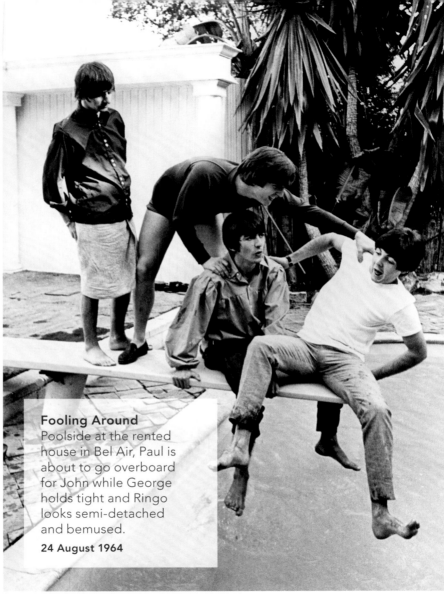

Fooling Around
Poolside at the rented house in Bel Air, Paul is about to go overboard for John while George holds tight and Ringo looks semi-detached and bemused.

24 August 1964

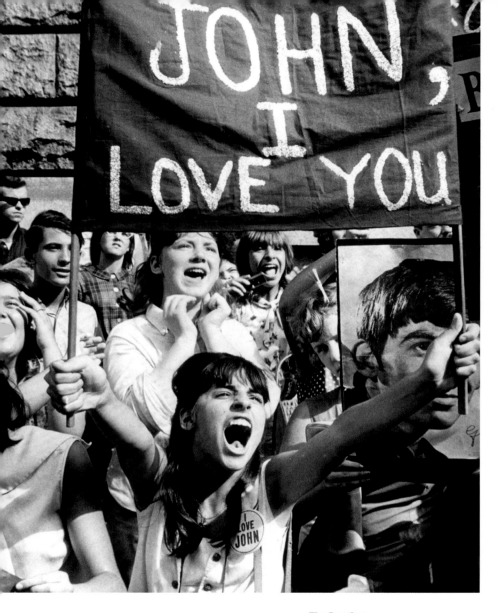

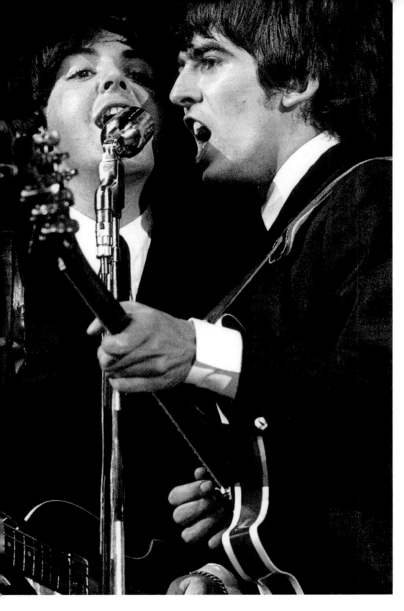

New York, New York

An audience of 16,000 came to New York's Forest Hills Stadium to see The Beatles play a 12 song set, starting with 'Twist and Shout' and ending with 'Long Tall Sally'.

28 August 1964

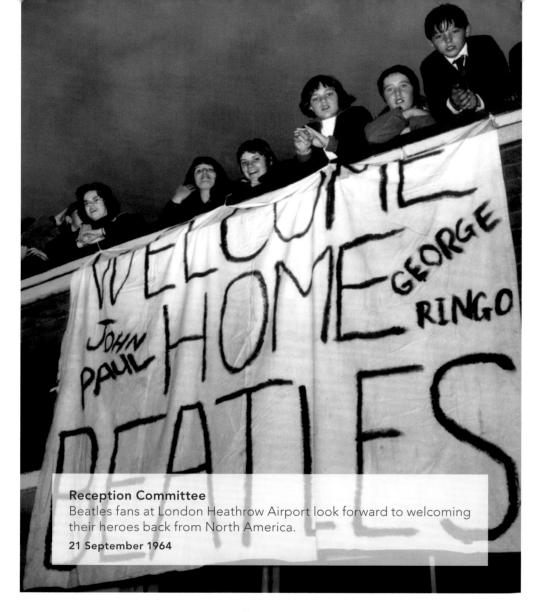

Reception Committee
Beatles fans at London Heathrow Airport look forward to welcoming their heroes back from North America.

21 September 1964

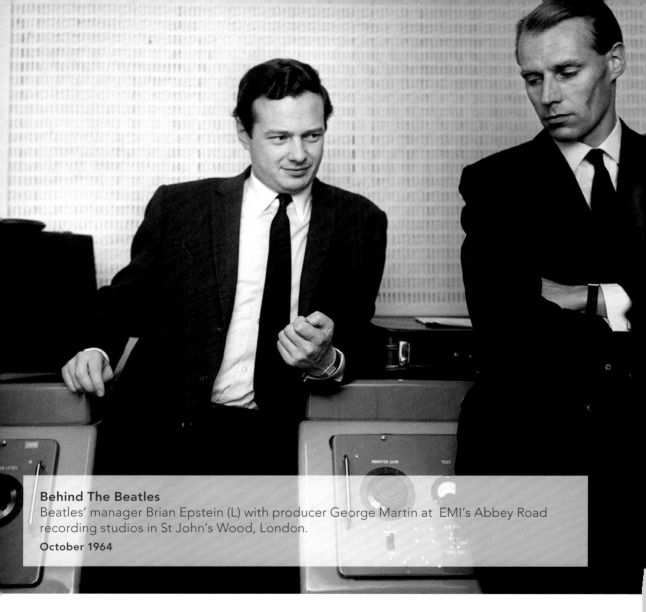

Behind The Beatles
Beatles' manager Brian Epstein (L) with producer George Martin at EMI's Abbey Road recording studios in St John's Wood, London.
October 1964

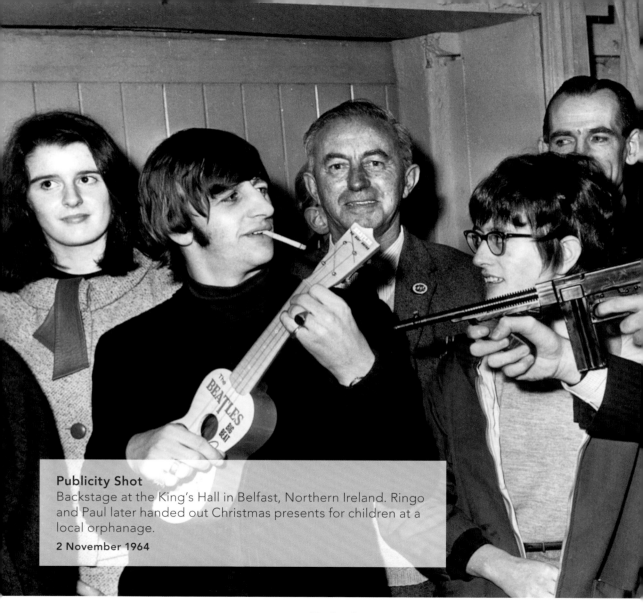

Publicity Shot
Backstage at the King's Hall in Belfast, Northern Ireland. Ringo and Paul later handed out Christmas presents for children at a local orphanage.
2 November 1964

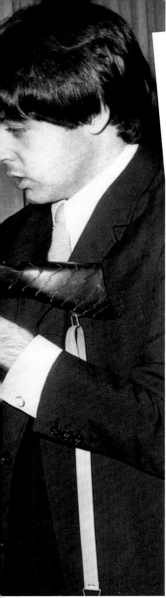

Best wishes from The Beatles

Ringo Starr

George Harrison

Paul McCartney

John Lennon

Full House
Getting one Beatle's autograph was something to boast about, but getting all of them on a single sheet of paper was no less than a triumph.

7 November 1964

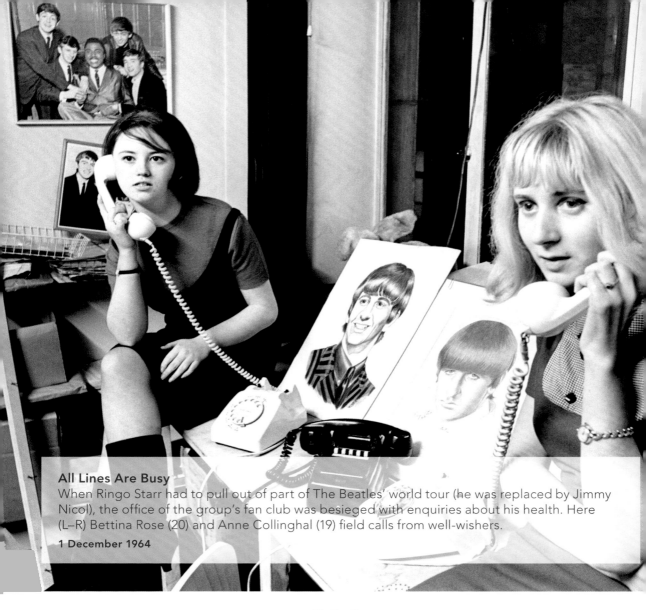

All Lines Are Busy

When Ringo Starr had to pull out of part of The Beatles' world tour (he was replaced by Jimmy Nicol), the office of the group's fan club was besieged with enquiries about his health. Here (L–R) Bettina Rose (20) and Anne Collinghal (19) field calls from well-wishers.

1 December 1964

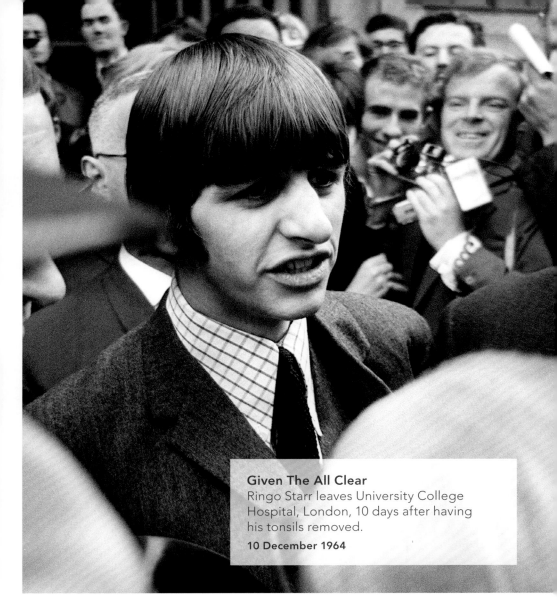

Given The All Clear
Ringo Starr leaves University College Hospital, London, 10 days after having his tonsils removed.

10 December 1964

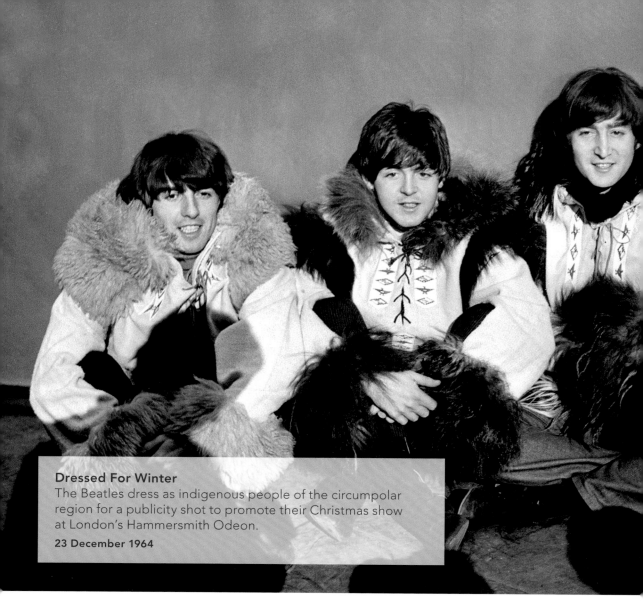

Dressed For Winter

The Beatles dress as indigenous people of the circumpolar region for a publicity shot to promote their Christmas show at London's Hammersmith Odeon.

23 December 1964

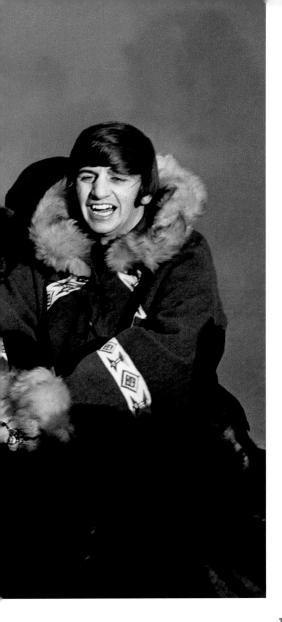

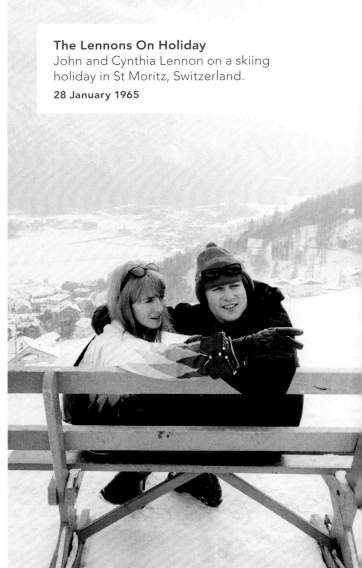

The Lennons On Holiday
John and Cynthia Lennon on a skiing
holiday in St Moritz, Switzerland.

28 January 1965

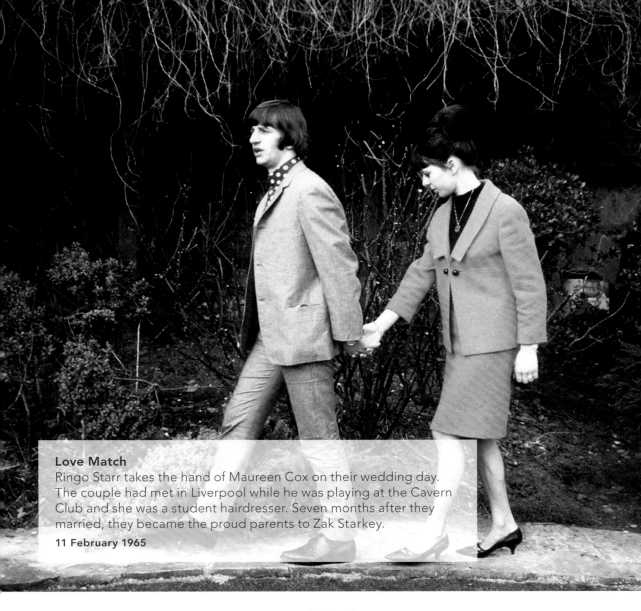

Love Match
Ringo Starr takes the hand of Maureen Cox on their wedding day.
The couple had met in Liverpool while he was playing at the Cavern
Club and she was a student hairdresser. Seven months after they
married, they became the proud parents to Zak Starkey.

11 February 1965

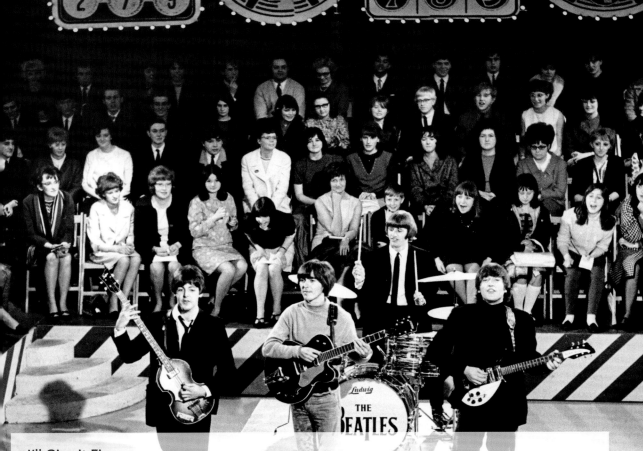

I'll Give It Five

The Beatles on *Thank Your Lucky Stars*. One of the best remembered parts of this ITV show was a pop panel on which stars and ordinary people marked newly released singles on a scale of one to five. The highest mark became a catchphrase, normally spoken in imitation of the strong Birmingham accent of Janice Nicholls, one of the judges.

28 March 1965

Vote Winning
The Beatles topped the bill at this year's annual *New Musical Express* poll winners' concert at the Empire Pool, Wembley. They played 'I Feel Fine', 'She's A Woman', 'Baby's in Black', 'Ticket To Ride' and 'Long Tall Sally'.

11 April 1965

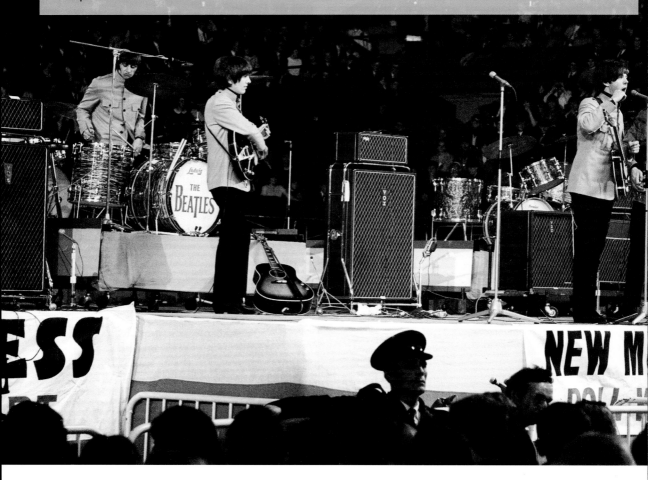

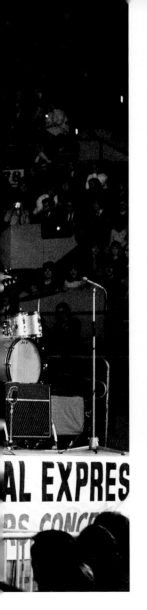
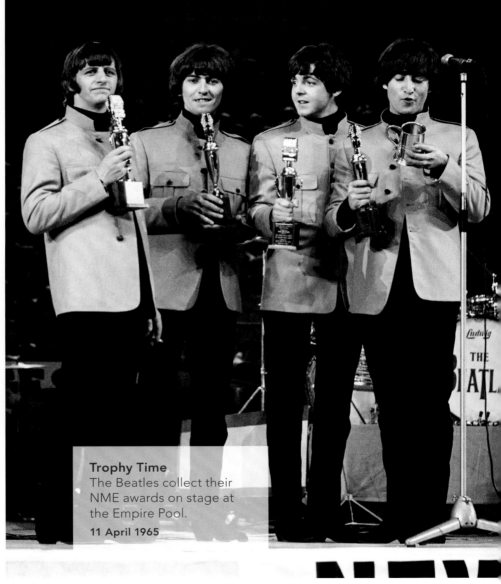

Trophy Time
The Beatles collect their
NME awards on stage at
the Empire Pool.
11 April 1965

The Beatles
139

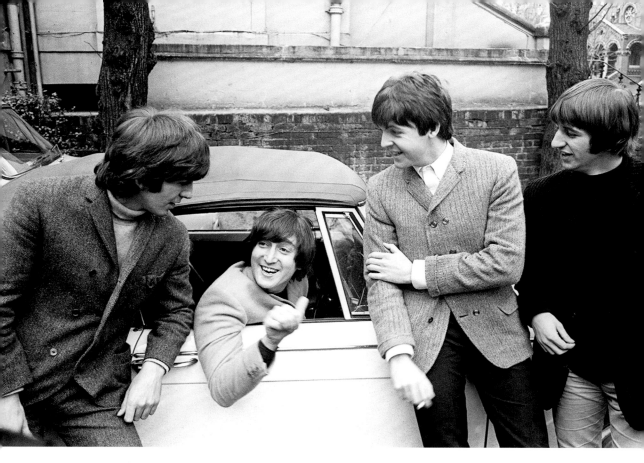

Lennon Without The L

When John Lennon passed his driving test, the other three Beatles joined him to celebrate the removal of the learner plates from his car.

15 February 1965

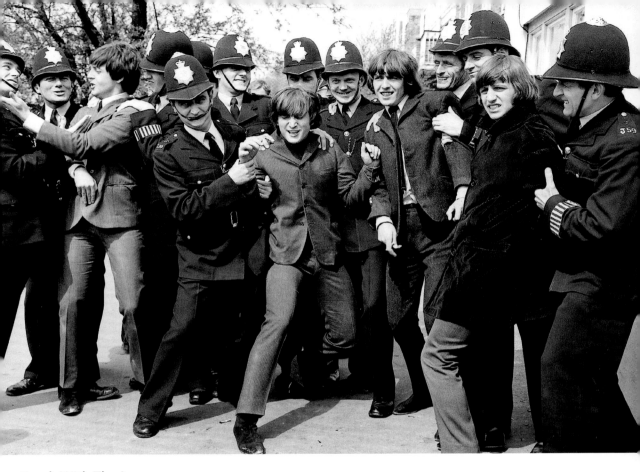

Brush With The Law

The Beatles filming a scene from *Help!* outside the City Barge pub in Chiswick, London. Everyone in the photo is an actor: no policemen were harmed in the shooting of this film.

24 April 1965

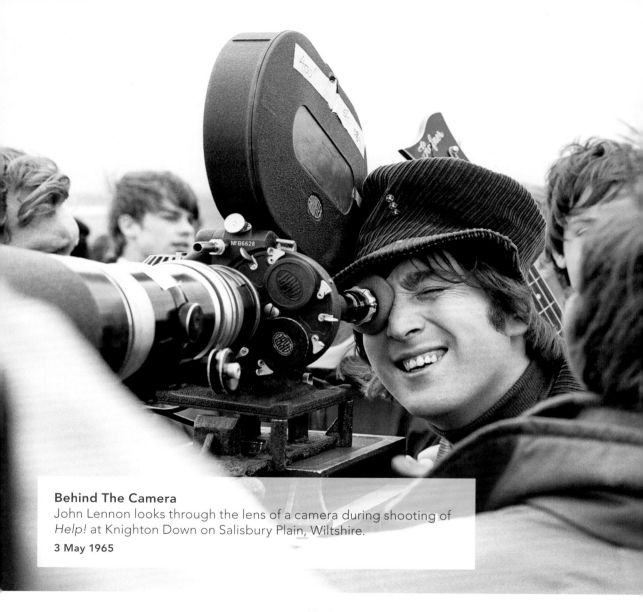

Behind The Camera
John Lennon looks through the lens of a camera during shooting of *Help!* at Knighton Down on Salisbury Plain, Wiltshire.

3 May 1965

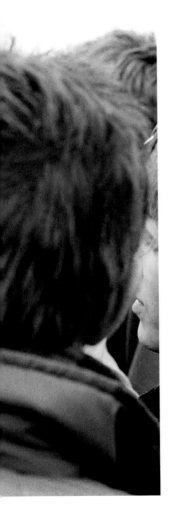
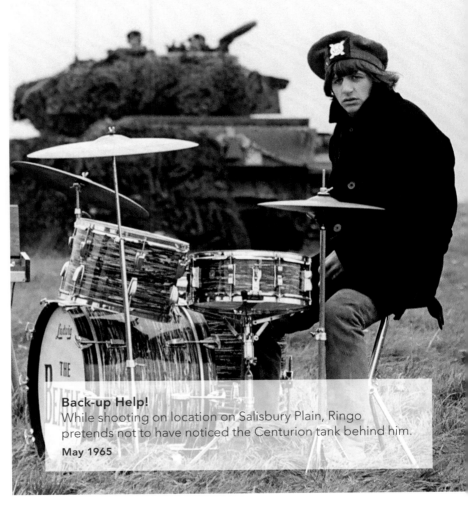

Back-up Help!
While shooting on location on Salisbury Plain, Ringo pretends not to have noticed the Centurion tank behind him.

May 1965

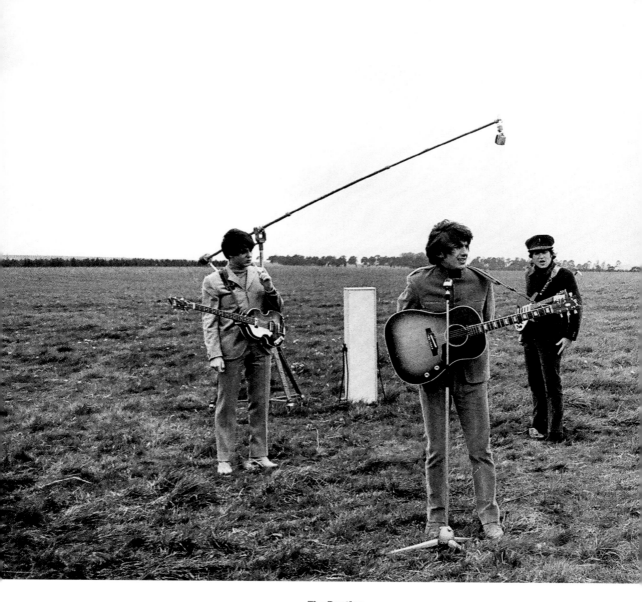

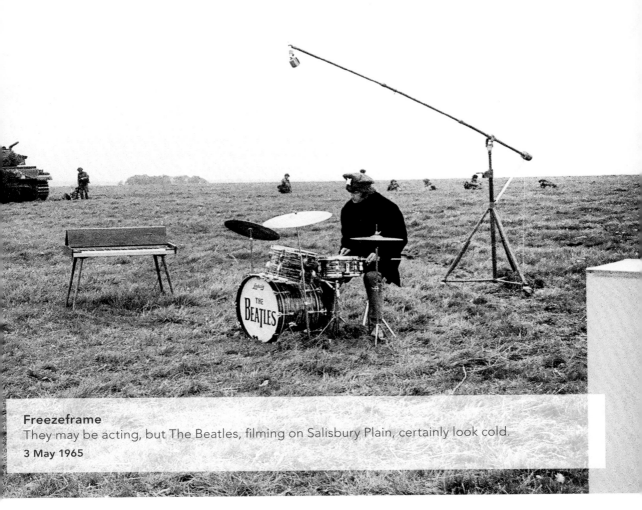

Freezeframe
They may be acting, but The Beatles, filming on Salisbury Plain, certainly look cold.
3 May 1965

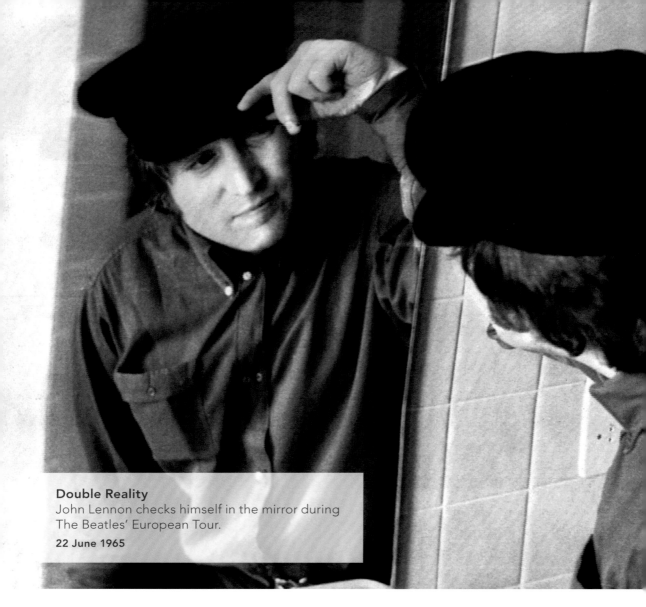

Double Reality
John Lennon checks himself in the mirror during
The Beatles' European Tour.

22 June 1965

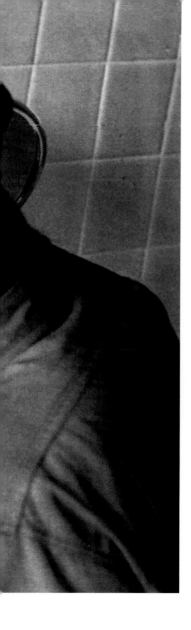

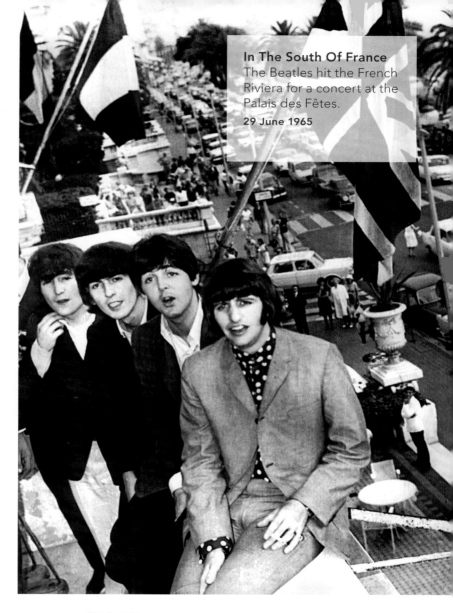

In The South Of France
The Beatles hit the French
Riviera for a concert at the
Palais des Fêtes.

29 June 1965

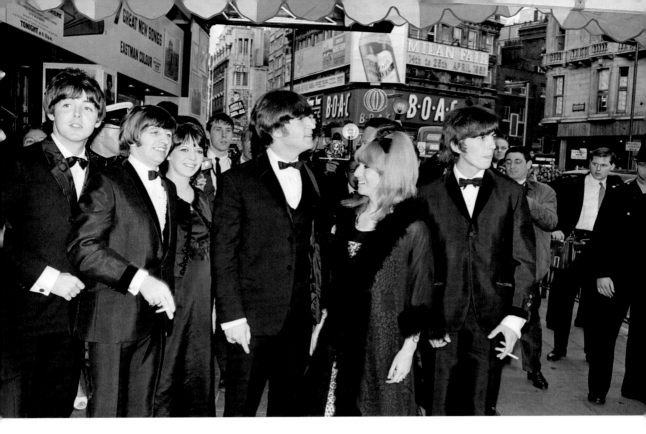

Dressed For The Occasion
Tuxed-up Beatles outside the London Pavilion in Piccadilly Circus before the royal première of *Help!* With them are Cynthia Lennon (second R) and Maureen Starkey (third L), who is dressed to hide her bump.

29 July 1965

Proud Father
Ringo tells the press about his son, Zak, born the previous day in Queen Charlotte's Hospital, London.

14 September 1965

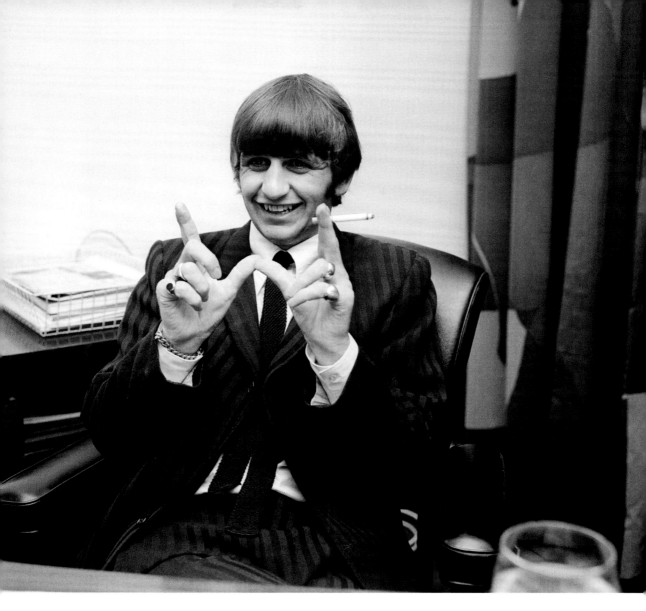

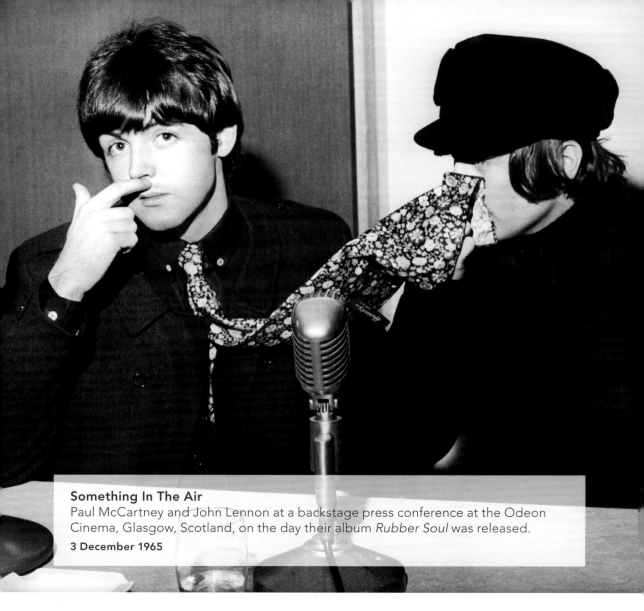

Something In The Air
Paul McCartney and John Lennon at a backstage press conference at the Odeon Cinema, Glasgow, Scotland, on the day their album *Rubber Soul* was released.

3 December 1965

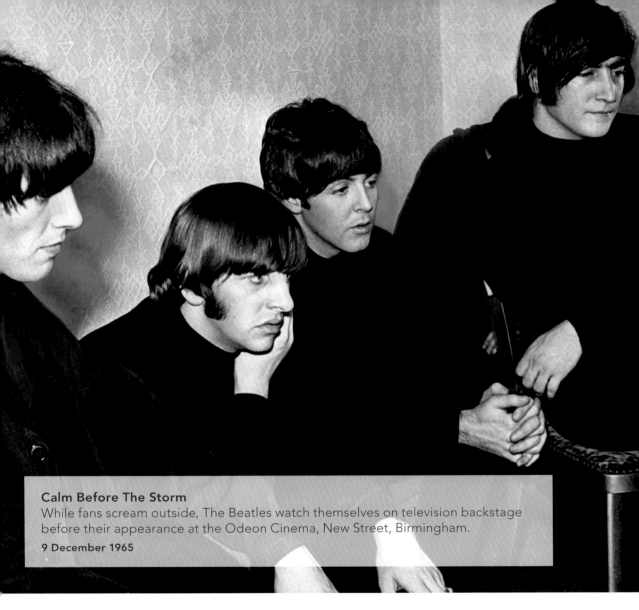

Calm Before The Storm

While fans scream outside, The Beatles watch themselves on television backstage before their appearance at the Odeon Cinema, New Street, Birmingham.

9 December 1965

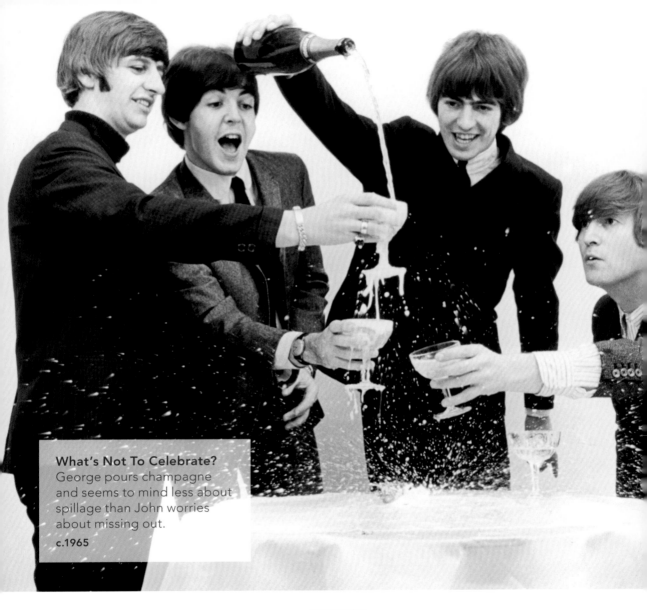

What's Not To Celebrate?
George pours champagne and seems to mind less about spillage than John worries about missing out.

c.1965

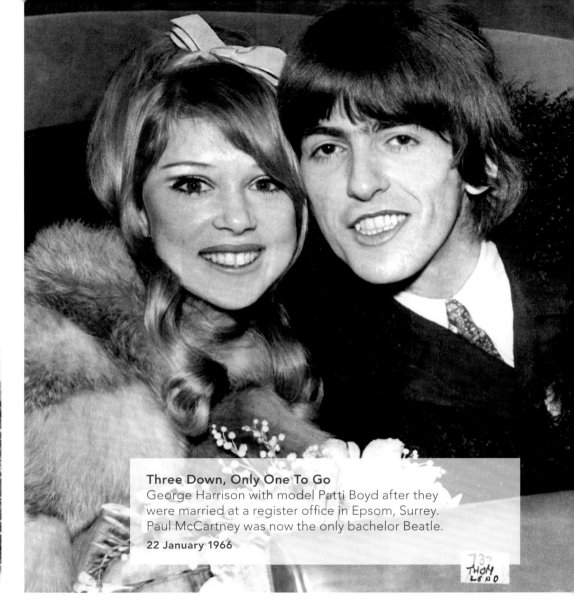

Three Down, Only One To Go
George Harrison with model Patti Boyd after they were married at a register office in Epsom, Surrey. Paul McCartney was now the only bachelor Beatle.

22 January 1966

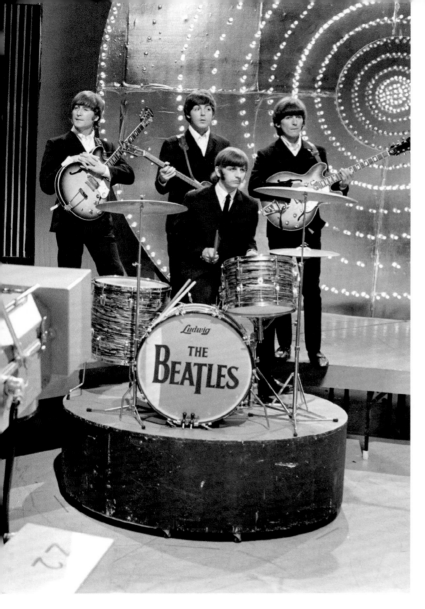
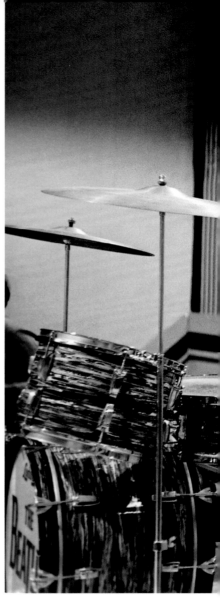

The Beatles
154

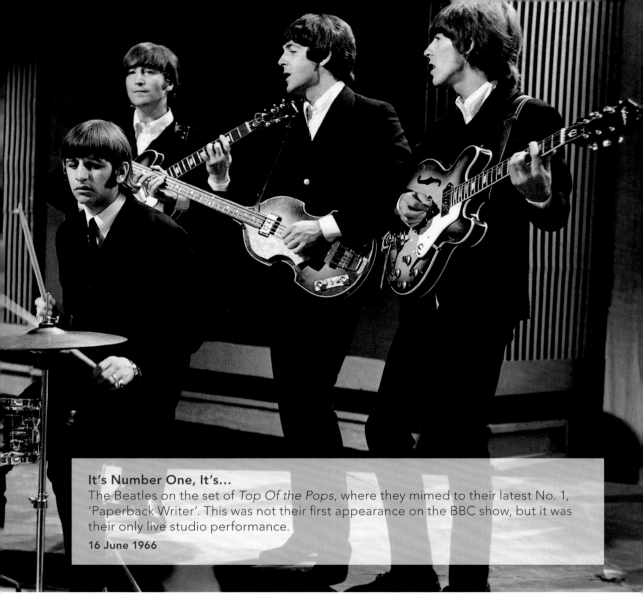

It's Number One, It's...
The Beatles on the set of *Top Of the Pops*, where they mimed to their latest No. 1, 'Paperback Writer'. This was not their first appearance on the BBC show, but it was their only live studio performance.

16 June 1966

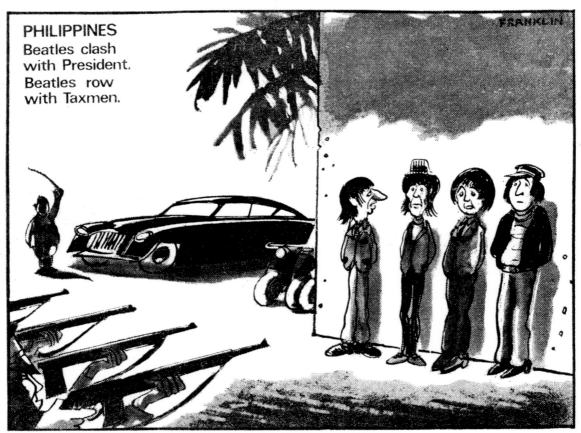

PHILIPPINES
Beatles clash
with President.
Beatles row
with Taxmen.

FRANKLIN

'*I thought it was the usual police escort*'

Diplomatic Incident

This Franklin cartoon from the *Daily Mirror* refers to both The Beatles' song 'Taxman' and to the hot diplomatic water in which the group landed after declining an invitation to a breakfast reception held by Philippines' President Marcos's wife Imelda. Hugely insulted, the ruler withdrew their police protection and they had to look out for themselves on their way to Manila Airport.

6 July 1966

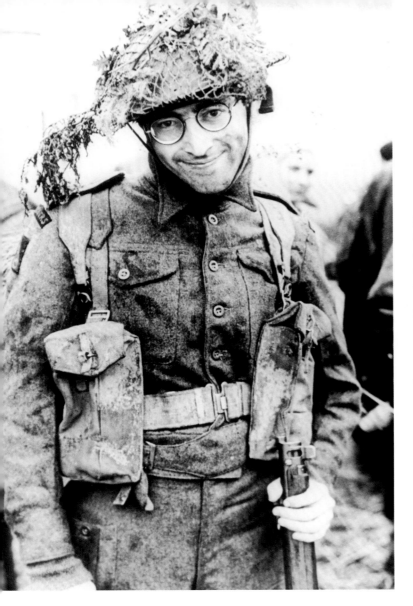

In Costume

On location in Germany, John Lennon dresses in army uniform for his role as Musketeer Gripweed in *How I Won The War*, a black comedy directed by Richard Lester, who had also directed *A Hard Day's Night* and *Help!*

6 September 1966

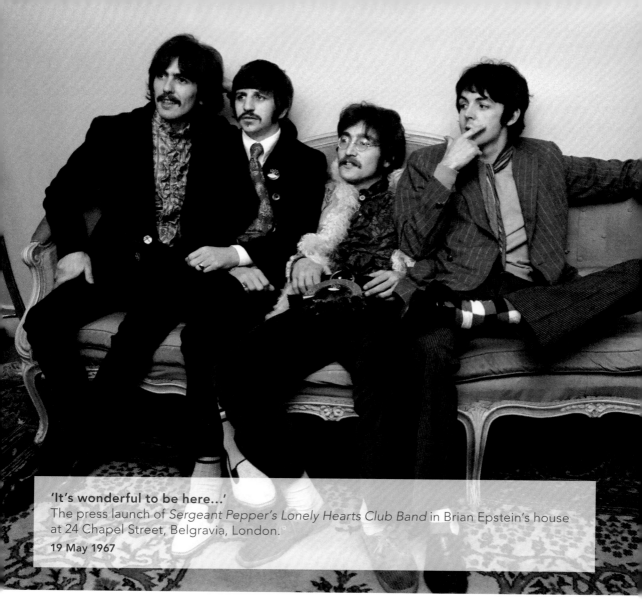

'It's wonderful to be here...'
The press launch of *Sergeant Pepper's Lonely Hearts Club Band* in Brian Epstein's house at 24 Chapel Street, Belgravia, London.
19 May 1967

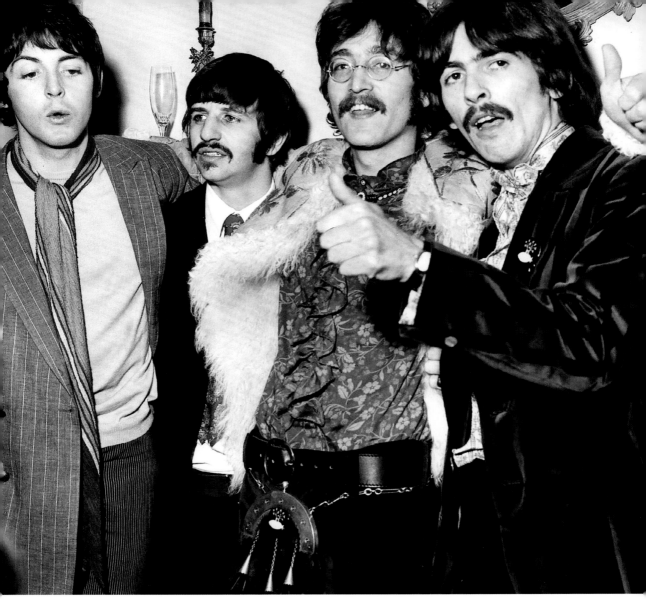

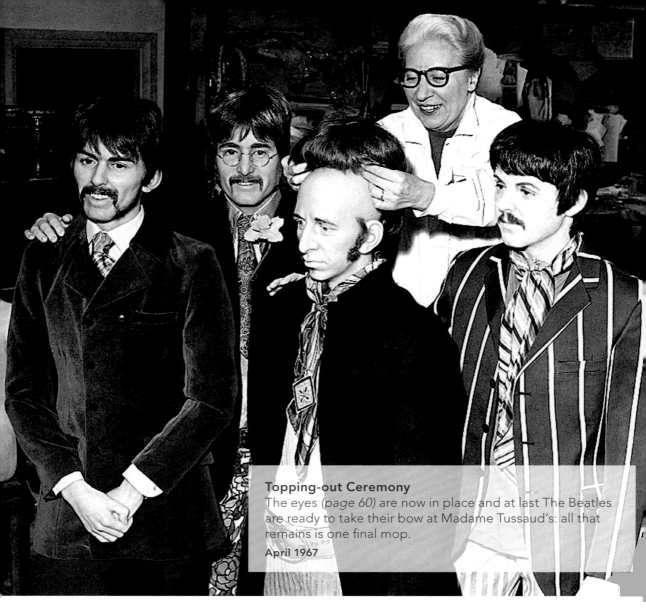

Topping-out Ceremony
The eyes *(page 60)* are now in place and at last The Beatles are ready to take their bow at Madame Tussaud's: all that remains is one final mop.

April 1967

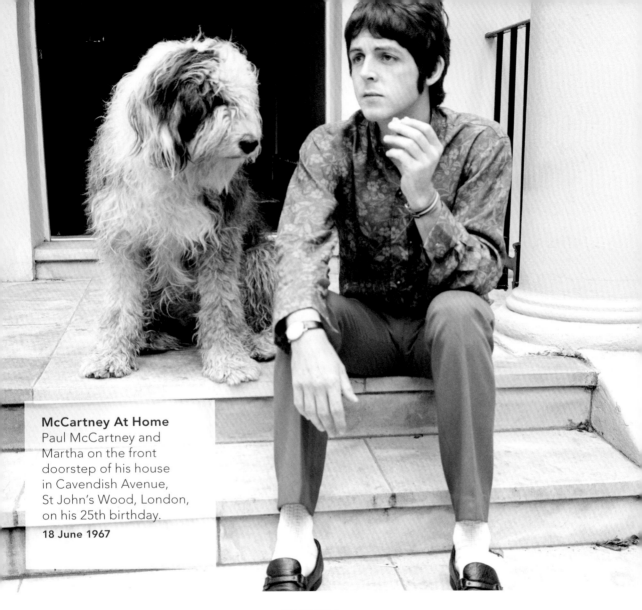

McCartney At Home
Paul McCartney and Martha on the front doorstep of his house in Cavendish Avenue, St John's Wood, London, on his 25th birthday.

18 June 1967

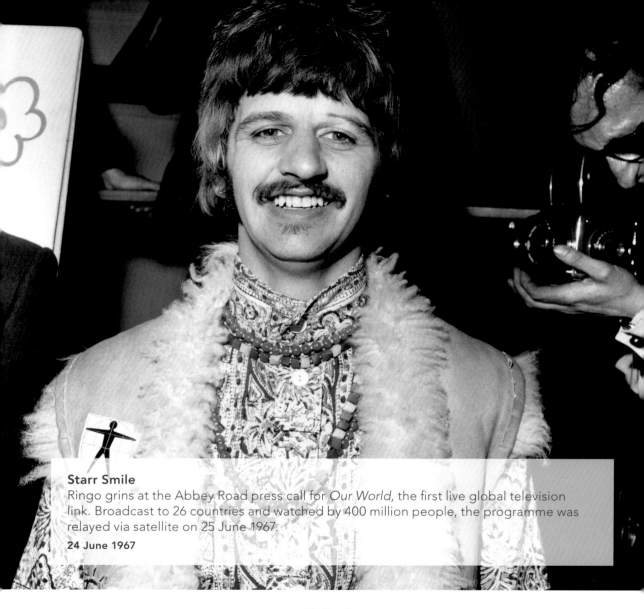

Starr Smile
Ringo grins at the Abbey Road press call for *Our World*, the first live global television link. Broadcast to 26 countries and watched by 400 million people, the programme was relayed via satellite on 25 June 1967.

24 June 1967

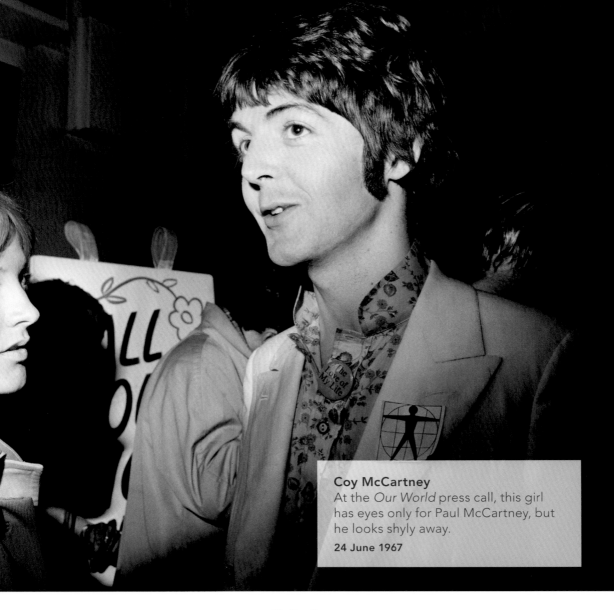

Coy McCartney

At the *Our World* press call, this girl has eyes only for Paul McCartney, but he looks shyly away.

24 June 1967

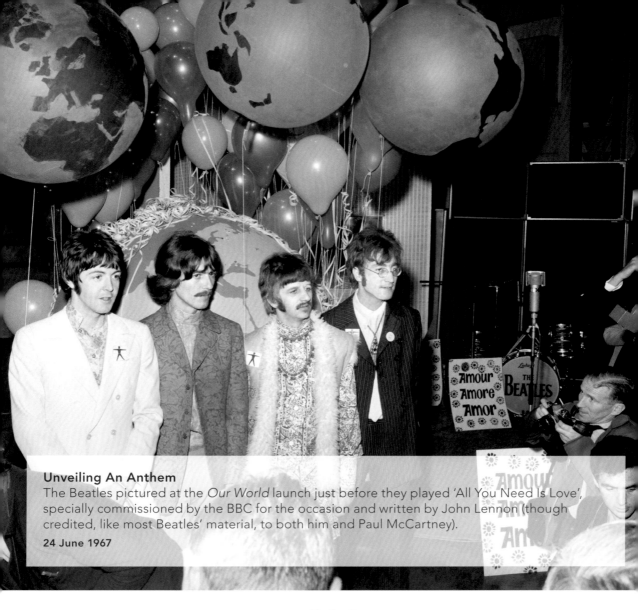

Unveiling An Anthem
The Beatles pictured at the *Our World* launch just before they played 'All You Need Is Love',
specially commissioned by the BBC for the occasion and written by John Lennon (though
credited, like most Beatles' material, to both him and Paul McCartney).

24 June 1967

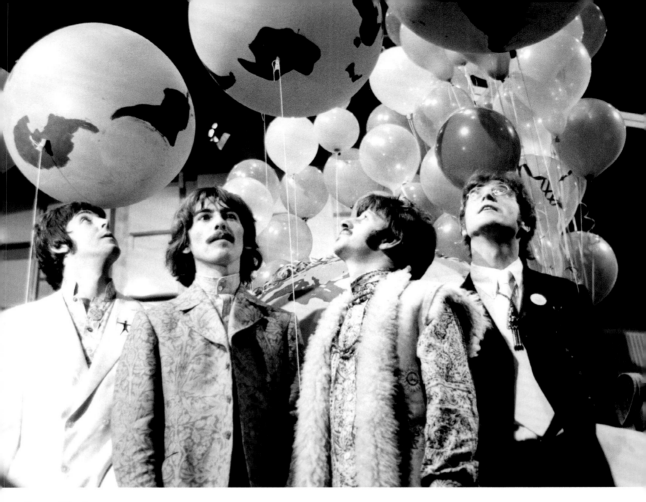

Press Shots
Newspaper photographers seemed to think that the balloons at the launch of *Our World* offered almost infinite creative possibilities. The Beatles obliged by striking slightly different poses every time the shutters clicked.

24 June 1967

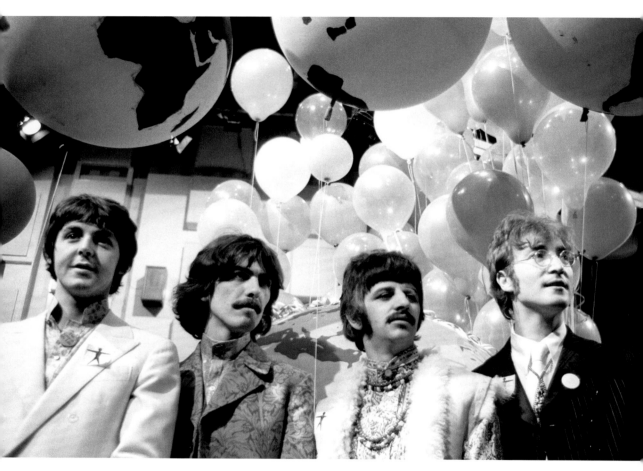

Unfazed
In this shot, the group make like they haven't noticed what's above their heads.
24 June 1967

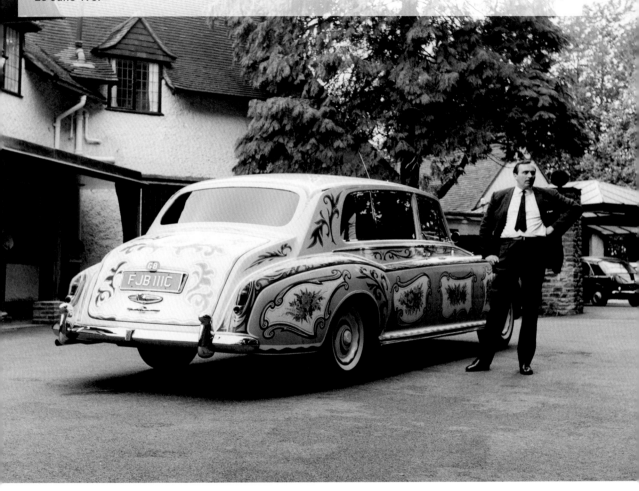

If You've Got It, Flaunt It
In the driveway of the Lennon residence in Surrey, a chauffeur stands beside the Beatle's Rolls-Royce Phantom, in yellow with psychedelic decals.

25 June 1967

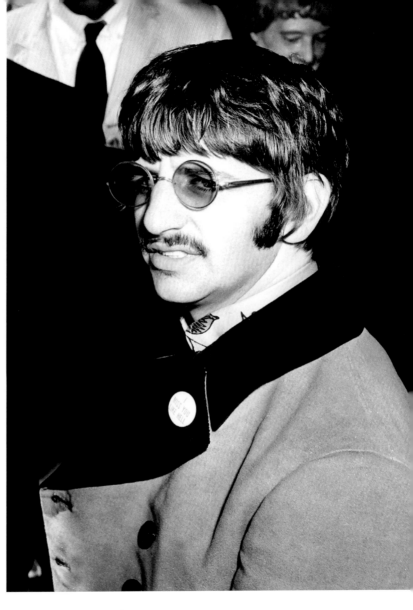

Second Son
Ringo Starr leaving Queen Charlotte's Hospital in London the day after Maureen gave birth to their second son, Jason Starkey.

20 August 1967

Spiritual Guru
Far right: Paul, George and John listen intently to the Maharishi Mahesh Yogi's philosophical teachings, when they met at London's Hilton Hotel.

24 August 1967

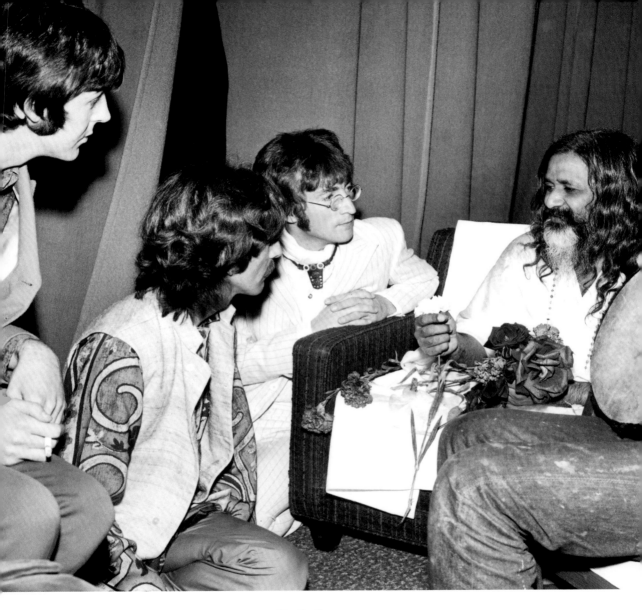

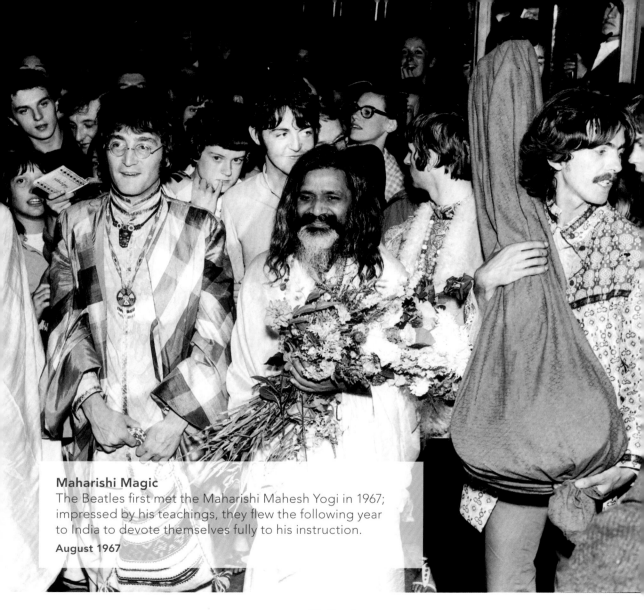

Maharishi Magic
The Beatles first met the Maharishi Mahesh Yogi in 1967; impressed by his teachings, they flew the following year to India to devote themselves fully to his instruction.

August 1967

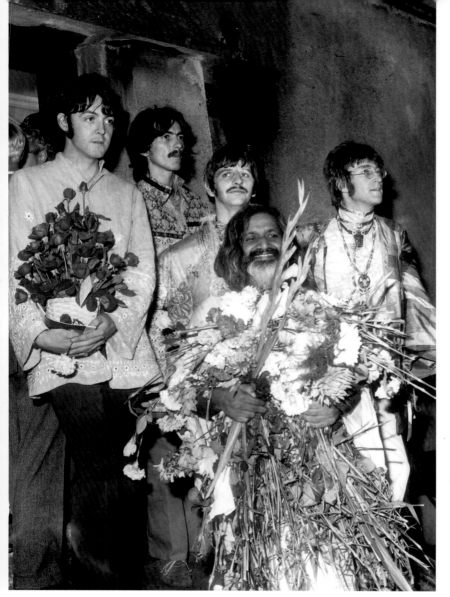

Flower Power
The Beatles travelled to Bangor, Wales, to attend a 10-day seminar given by the Maharishi.

August 1967

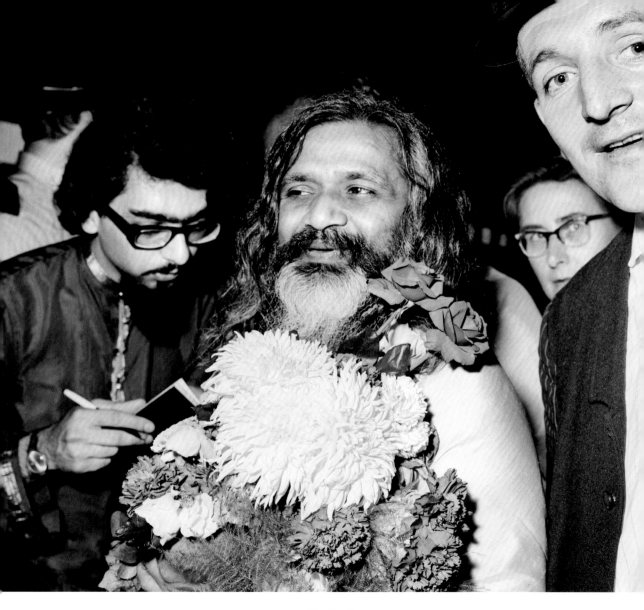

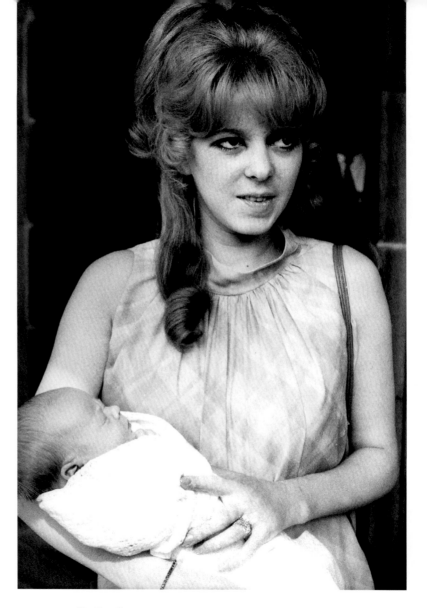

Spiritual Trip
Left: Maharishi Mahesh
Yogi at Euston Station
waiting to leave for his
summer school in Wales,
which was attended by
members of The Beatles
and The Rolling Stones.
25 August 1967

Baby Of A Rich Man
Maureen Starr leaves hospital
with Jason the new Beatle
baby, now one week old.
26 August 1967

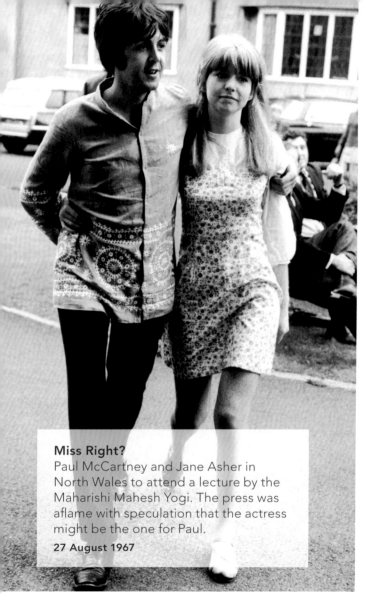

Miss Right?
Paul McCartney and Jane Asher in
North Wales to attend a lecture by the
Maharishi Mahesh Yogi. The press was
aflame with speculation that the actress
might be the one for Paul.

27 August 1967

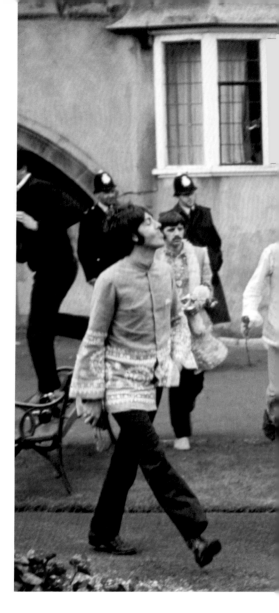

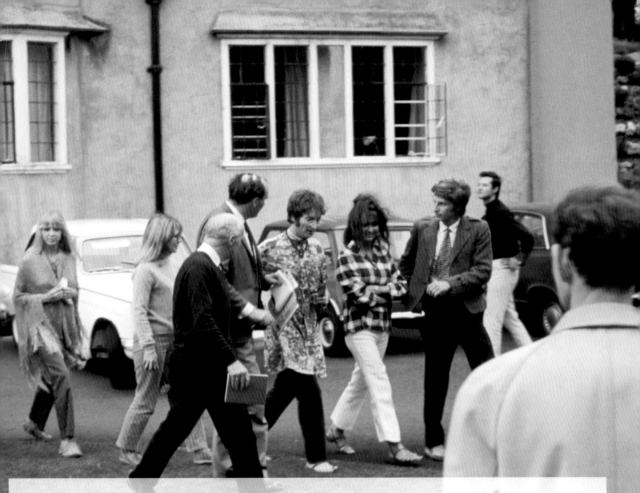

Heartbreak
Having just learned of the death of Brian Epstein, The Beatles cut short their Welsh sojourn and hurry back to London.

27 August 1967

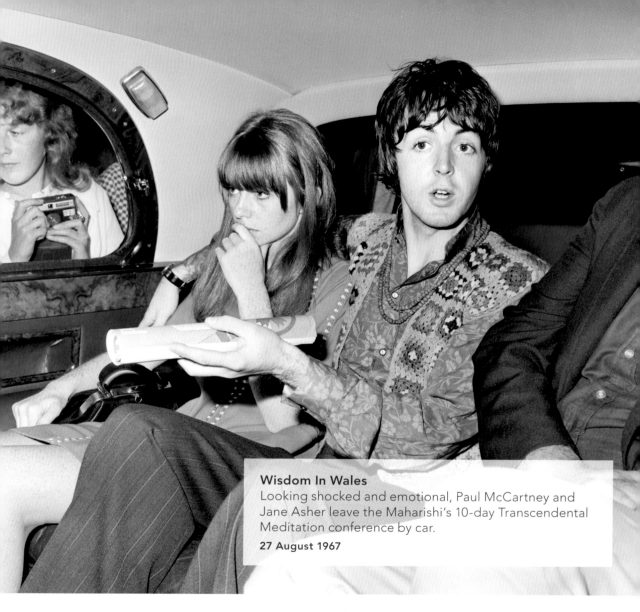

Wisdom In Wales
Looking shocked and emotional, Paul McCartney and Jane Asher leave the Maharishi's 10-day Transcendental Meditation conference by car.

27 August 1967

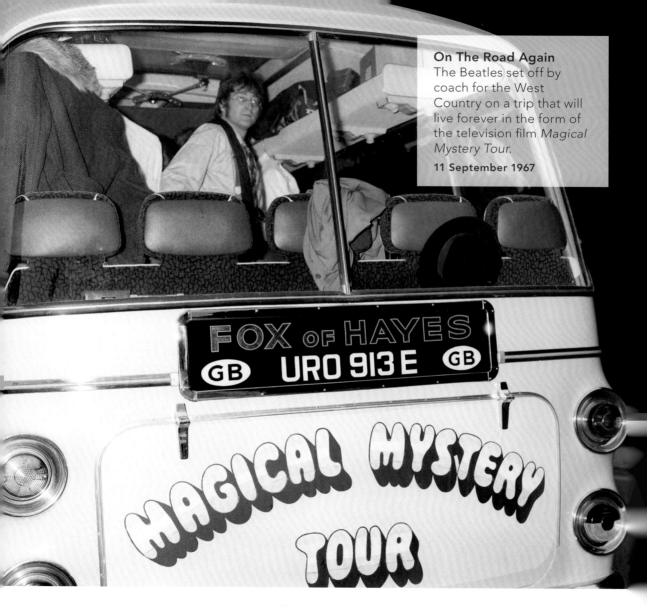

FOX OF HAYES
GB URO 913 E GB

MAGICAL MYSTERY TOUR

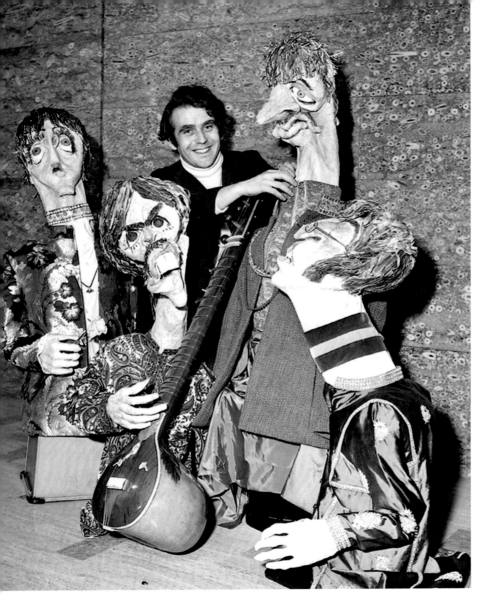

Model Citizens
Left: Gerald Scarfe with papier-mâché puppets of The Beatles, which he produced for the cover of *Time* magazine. The cartoonist later went on to marry McCartney's ex-girlfriend Jane Asher.

19 September 1967

Movie Première
George Harrison and wife Patti Boyd arriving at the London première of *How I Won the Wa* (*see page 155*), which features fellow Beatle John Lennon

18 October 1967

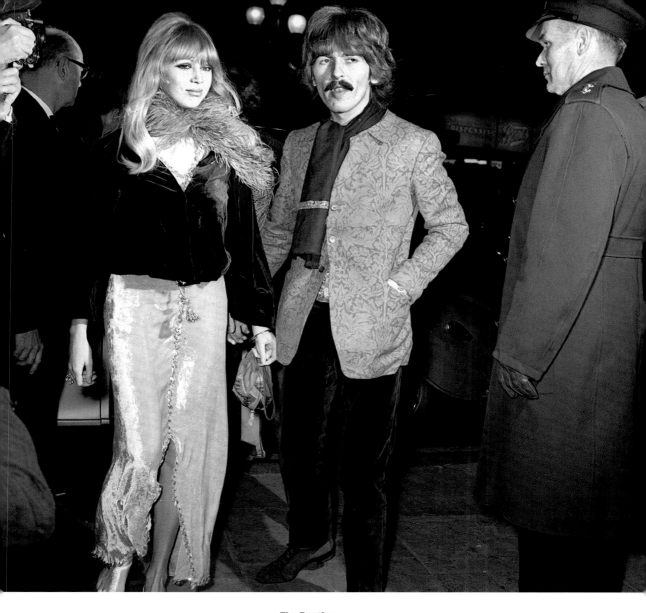

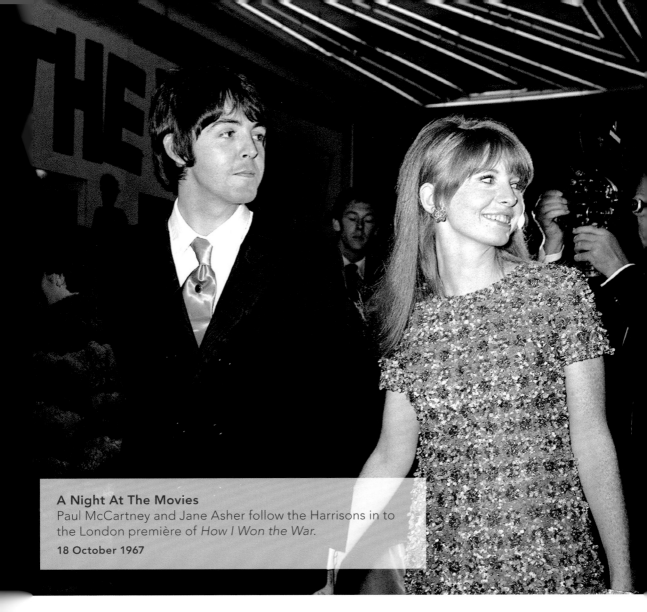

A Night At The Movies
Paul McCartney and Jane Asher follow the Harrisons in to the London première of *How I Won the War*.

18 October 1967

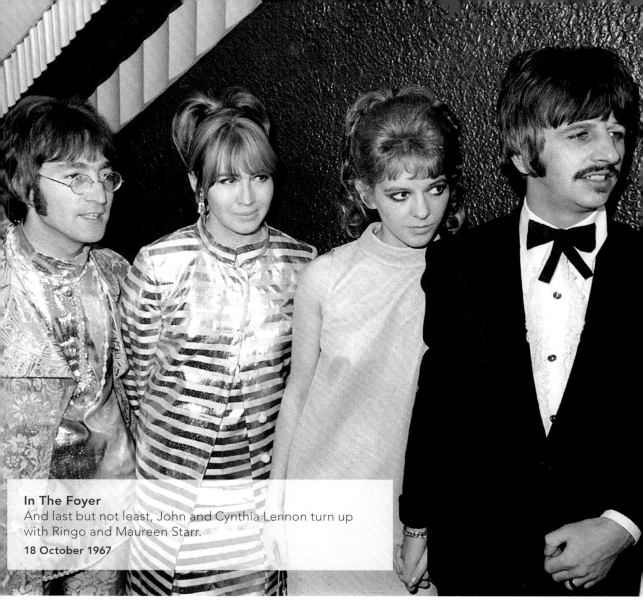

In The Foyer
And last but not least, John and Cynthia Lennon turn up
with Ringo and Maureen Starr.

18 October 1967

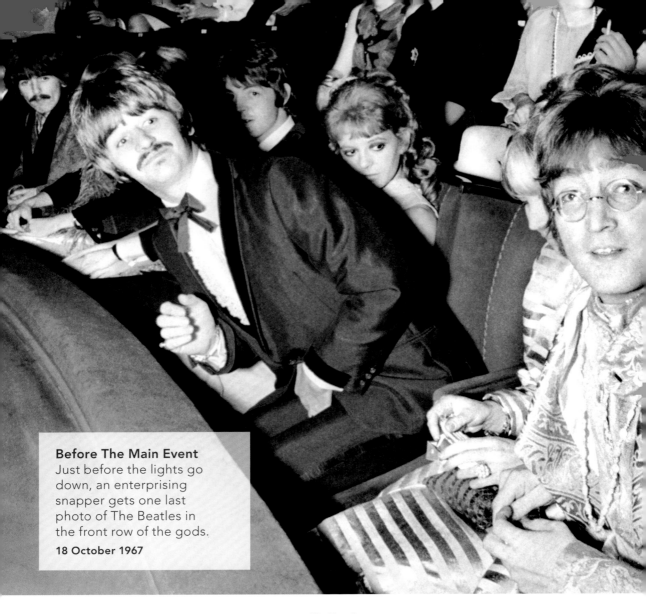

Before The Main Event
Just before the lights go down, an enterprising snapper gets one last photo of The Beatles in the front row of the gods.

18 October 1967

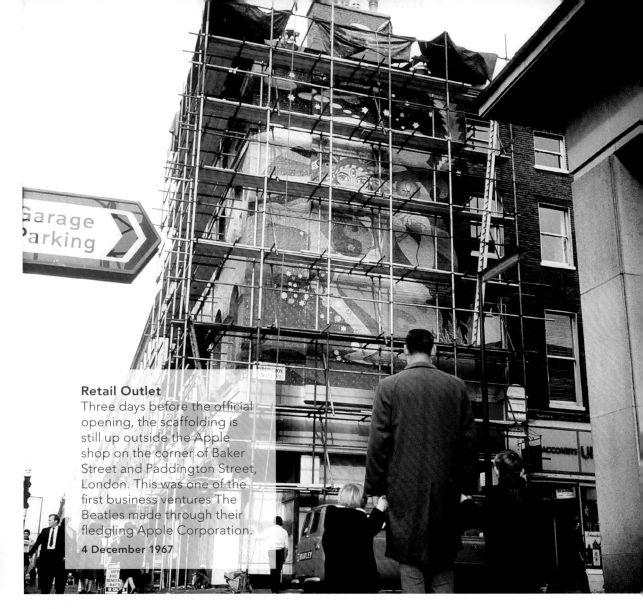

Retail Outlet

Three days before the official opening, the scaffolding is still up outside the Apple shop on the corner of Baker Street and Paddington Street, London. This was one of the first business ventures The Beatles made through their fledgling Apple Corporation.

4 December 1967

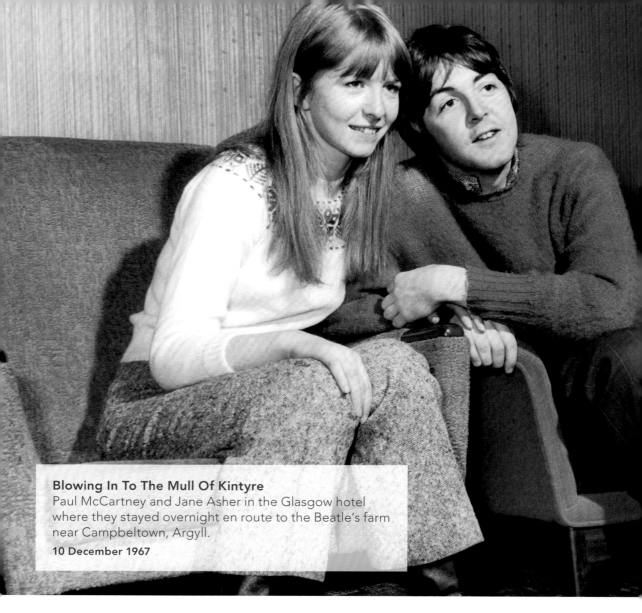

Blowing In To The Mull Of Kintyre
Paul McCartney and Jane Asher in the Glasgow hotel
where they stayed overnight en route to the Beatle's farm
near Campbeltown, Argyll.

10 December 1967

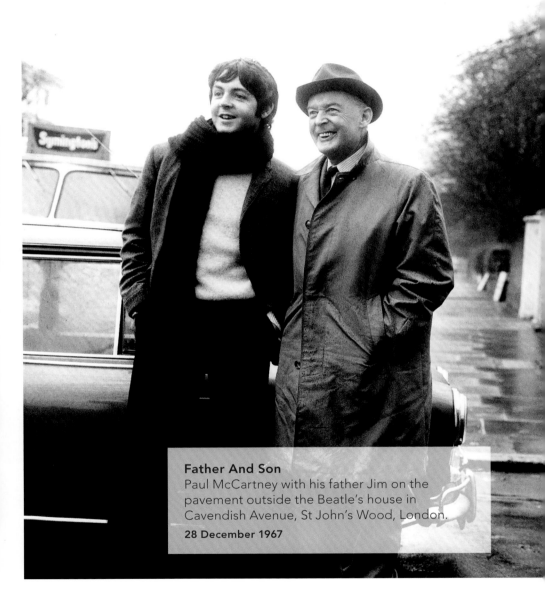

Father And Son

Paul McCartney with his father Jim on the pavement outside the Beatle's house in Cavendish Avenue, St John's Wood, London.

28 December 1967

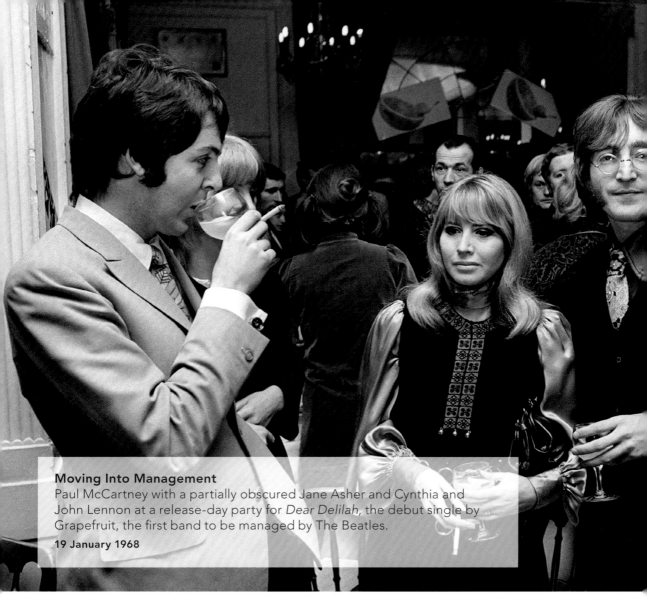

Moving Into Management

Paul McCartney with a partially obscured Jane Asher and Cynthia and John Lennon at a release-day party for *Dear Delilah*, the debut single by Grapefruit, the first band to be managed by The Beatles.

19 January 1968

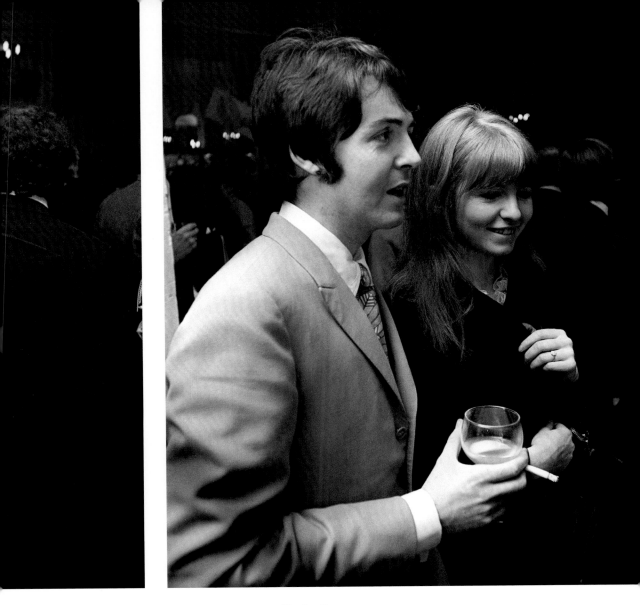

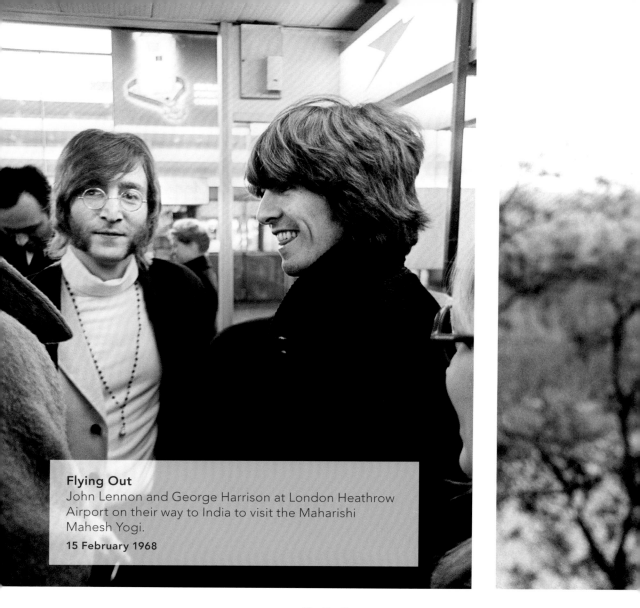

Flying Out
John Lennon and George Harrison at London Heathrow Airport on their way to India to visit the Maharishi Mahesh Yogi.

15 February 1968

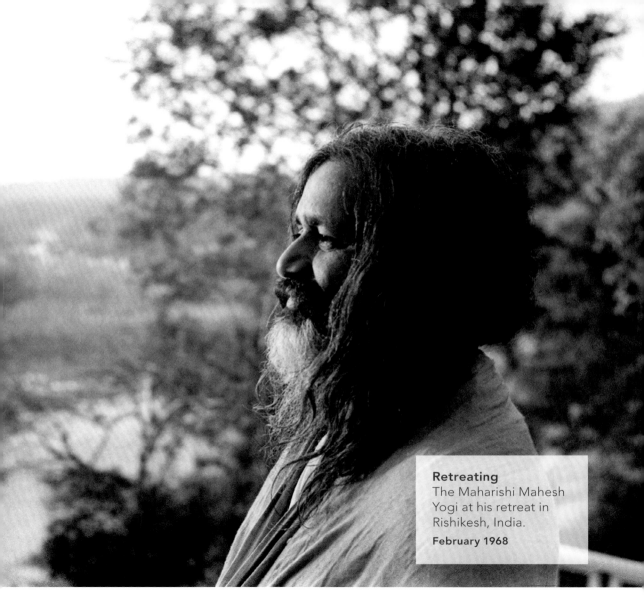

Retreating
The Maharishi Mahesh Yogi at his retreat in Rishikesh, India.

February 1968

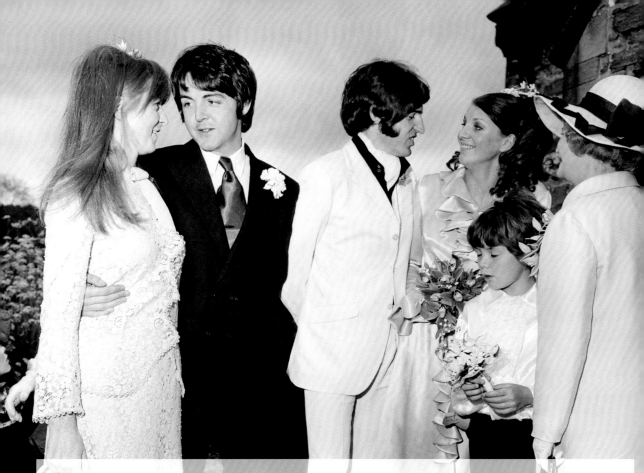

Tying The Knot

Paul McCartney and Jane Asher in Carrog, North Wales, at the wedding of Angela Fishwick to Paul's younger brother Mike, who under the stage name Mike McGear was a member of The Scaffold, who would have a No. 1 single the following year with 'Lily the Pink'.

8 June 1968

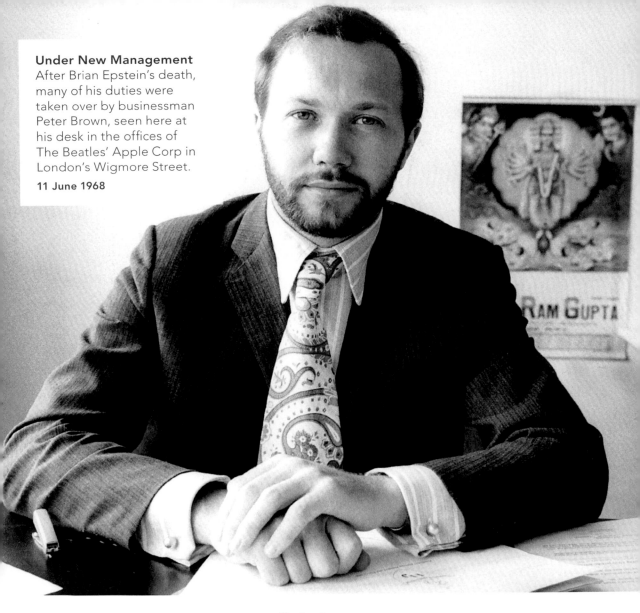

Under New Management
After Brian Epstein's death, many of his duties were taken over by businessman Peter Brown, seen here at his desk in the offices of The Beatles' Apple Corp in London's Wigmore Street.

11 June 1968

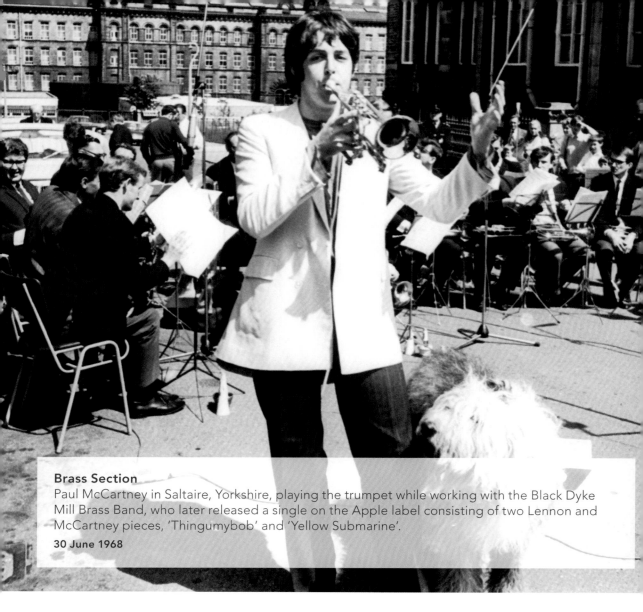

Brass Section
Paul McCartney in Saltaire, Yorkshire, playing the trumpet while working with the Black Dyke Mill Brass Band, who later released a single on the Apple label consisting of two Lennon and McCartney pieces, 'Thingumybob' and 'Yellow Submarine'.

30 June 1968

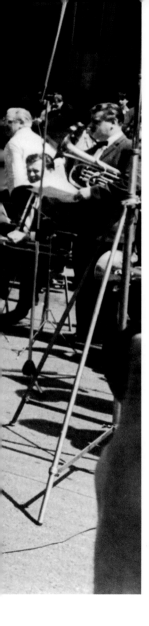

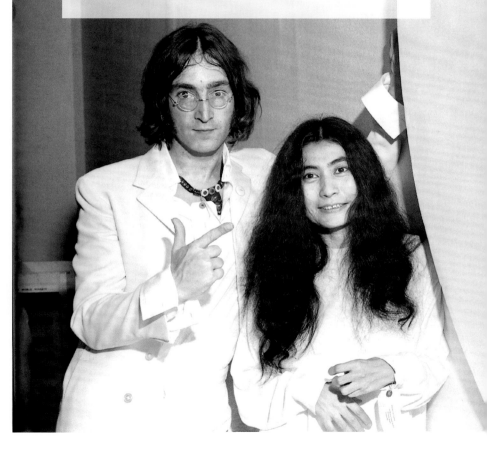

Art Lovers
John Lennon first met Yoko Ono in November 1966. As his marriage to Cynthia foundered, he became more involved with the Japanese artist and they opened an exhibition of her work, entitled *You Are Here*, at a gallery in London's West End.

1 July 1968

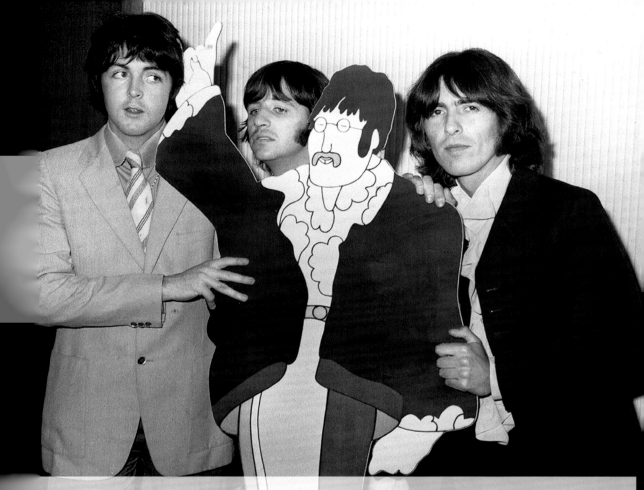

Cardboard Lennon
A week before the UK release of *Yellow Submarine*, Paul, Ringo and George pose beside a cardboard cut-out of John that featured in the film.

9 July 1968

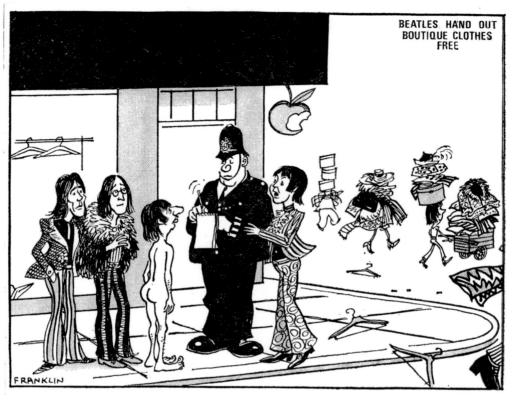

"Ringo got a bit carried away, officer.."

Everything Must Go

When The Beatles closed their Apple boutique *(see page 181)*, they announced that all the stock would be given away rather than sold off cheaply. Hundreds queued all night to take advantage of the offer, and the chaos that ensued inspired this Franklin cartoon in the following morning's *Daily Mirror*.

1 August 1968

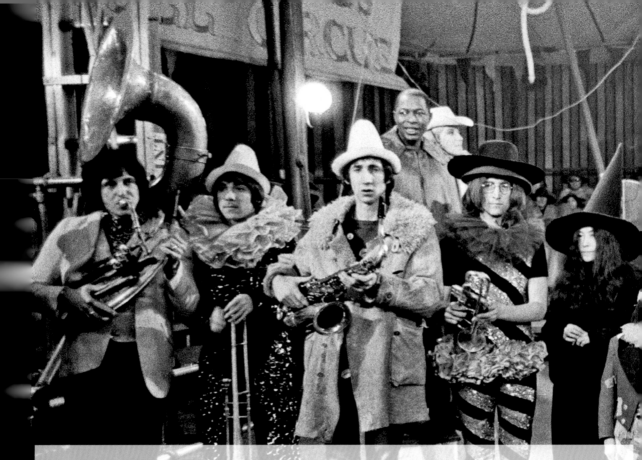

The Rolling Stones Rock 'n' Roll Circus
This extravaganza – two concerts on a circus stage in Stonebridge Park near Wembley, Middlesex – featured a host of stars including (L–R): John Entwistle, Keith Moon and Pete Townshend of The Who; John Lennon and Yoko Ono (now his fiancée); Keith Richards, Mick Jagger, Brian Jones and Bill Wyman (The Rolling Stones); Eric Clapton and Marianne Faithfull.

11 December 1968

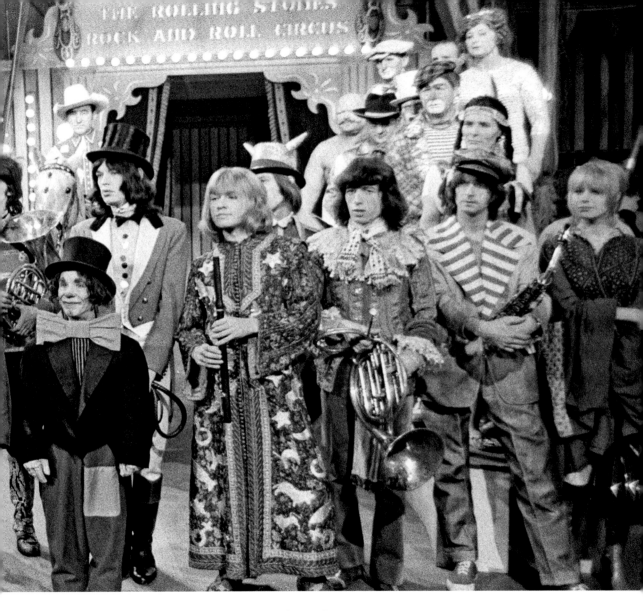

THE ROLLING STONES
ROCK AND ROLL CIRCUS

The Beatles
197

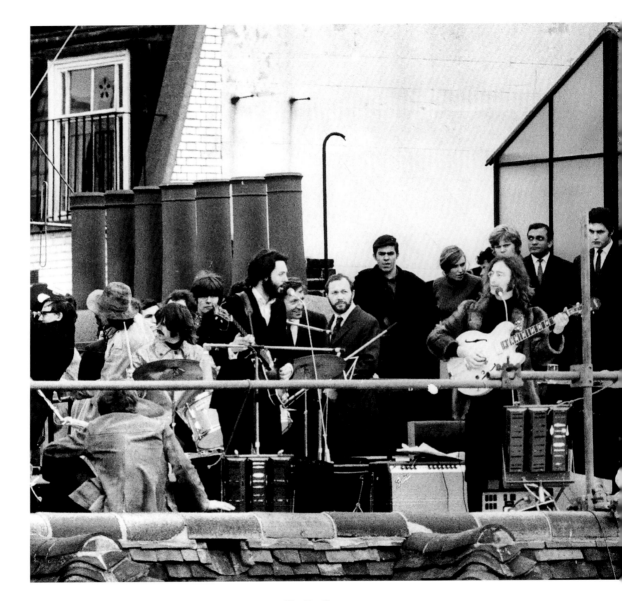

The Beatles
198

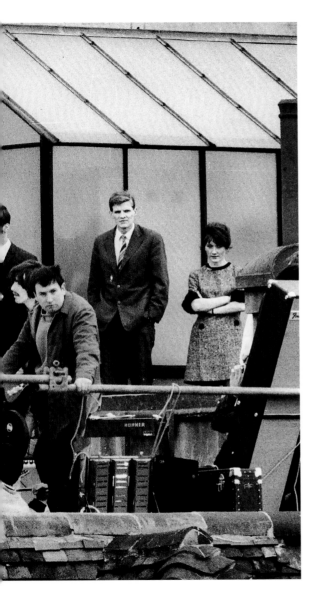

The Rooftop Concert
The Beatles' last-ever live performance, an unannounced gig on top of their Apple headquarters in London's Savile Row.

30 January 1969

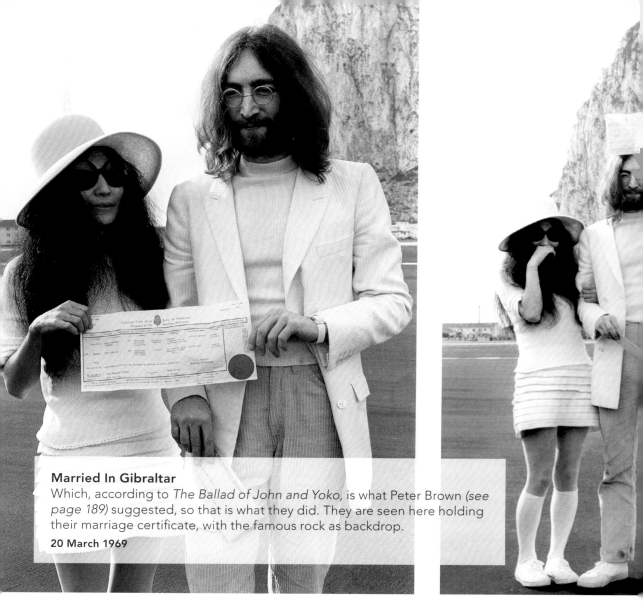

Married In Gibraltar
Which, according to *The Ballad of John and Yoko*, is what Peter Brown (*see page 189*) suggested, so that is what they did. They are seen here holding their marriage certificate, with the famous rock as backdrop.

20 March 1969

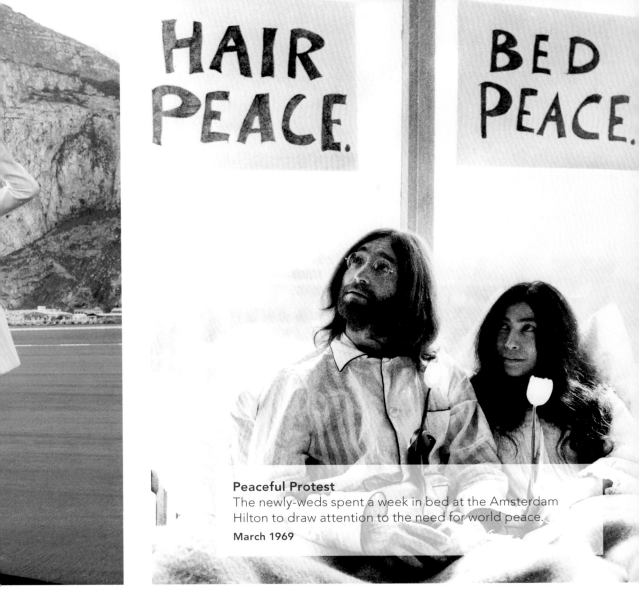

HAIR PEACE.

BED PEACE.

Peaceful Protest
The newly-weds spent a week in bed at the Amsterdam
Hilton to draw attention to the need for world peace.
March 1969

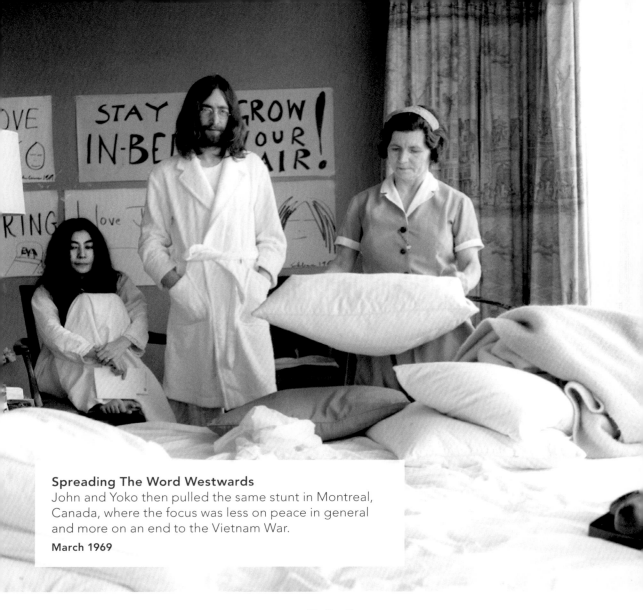

Spreading The Word Westwards

John and Yoko then pulled the same stunt in Montreal, Canada, where the focus was less on peace in general and more on an end to the Vietnam War.

March 1969

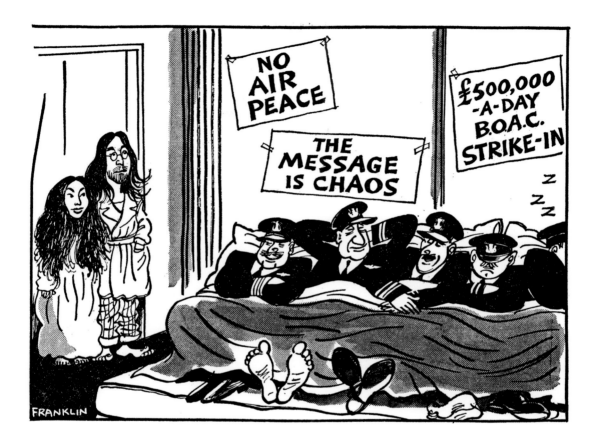

Bedroom Antics

This Franklin cartoon from the *Daily Mirror* takes a sideways look at two of the big news items of the day: John and Yoko in bed and a BOAC pilots' strike.

1 April 1969

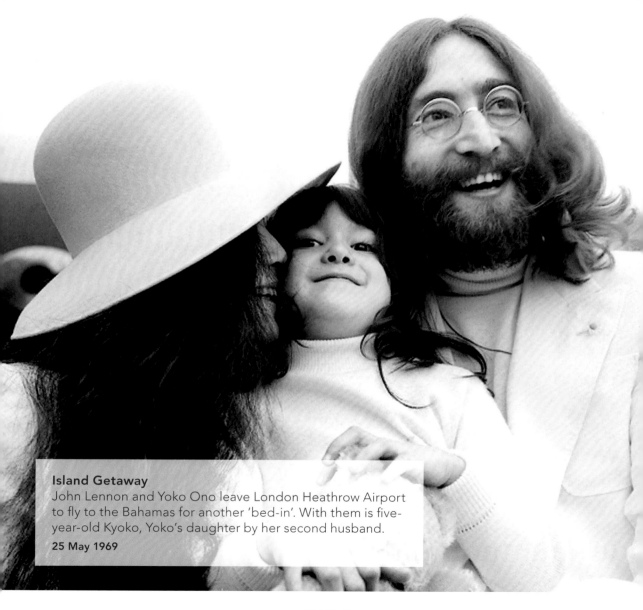

Island Getaway

John Lennon and Yoko Ono leave London Heathrow Airport to fly to the Bahamas for another 'bed-in'. With them is five-year-old Kyoko, Yoko's daughter by her second husband.

25 May 1969

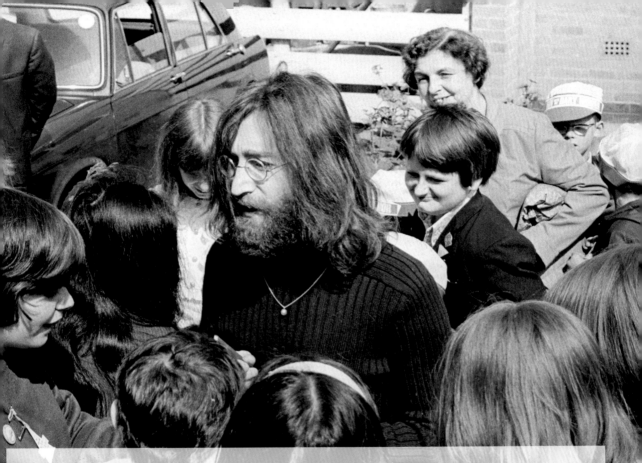

Trouble Ahead

John Lennon and Yoko Ono greeting fans before a trip up to Durness, Scotland, in their Austin Maxi with his son Julian and her daughter Kyoko. Unfortunately the journey ended 40 miles (64km) from their intended destination in a ditch near Tongue. John was driving on a single-track road and swerved to avoid a confused German driver coming the other way.

27 June 1969

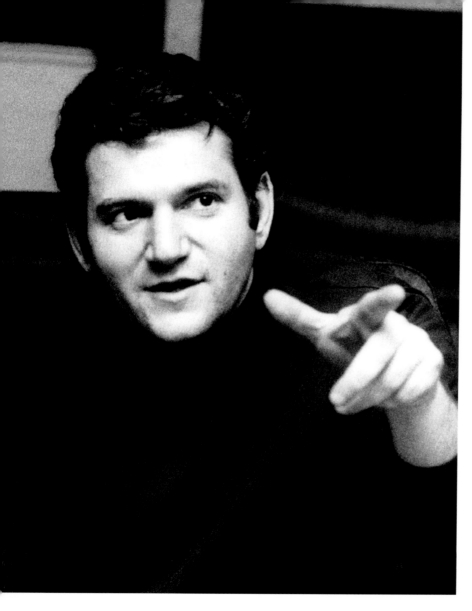

Allen Klein

Without Brian Epstein to guide them, The Beatles did not manage their money well. The Apple Corp was heading for disaster when Lennon, Harrison and Starr brought in Allen Klein to save them. McCartney, however, was unimpressed by the American businessman and never signed up with him.

1 July 1969

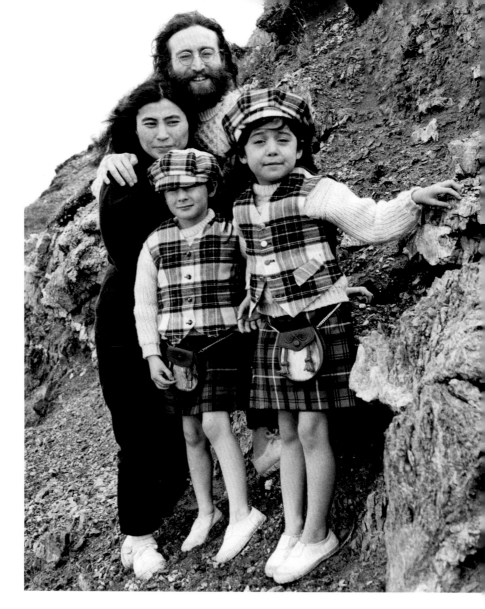

Highland Fling
John Lennon and Yoko
Ono stand on a Scottish
mountainside with
his son Julian and her
daughter Kyoko.
2 July 1969

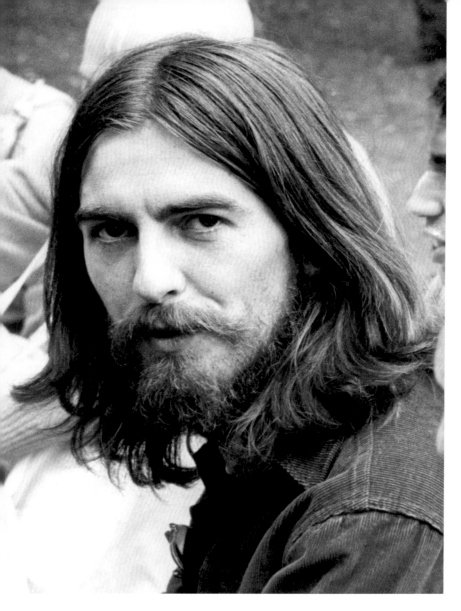
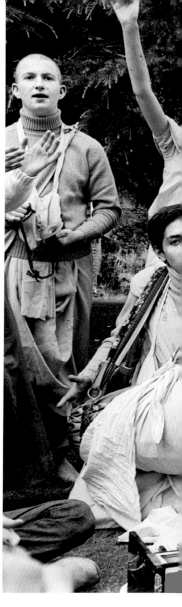

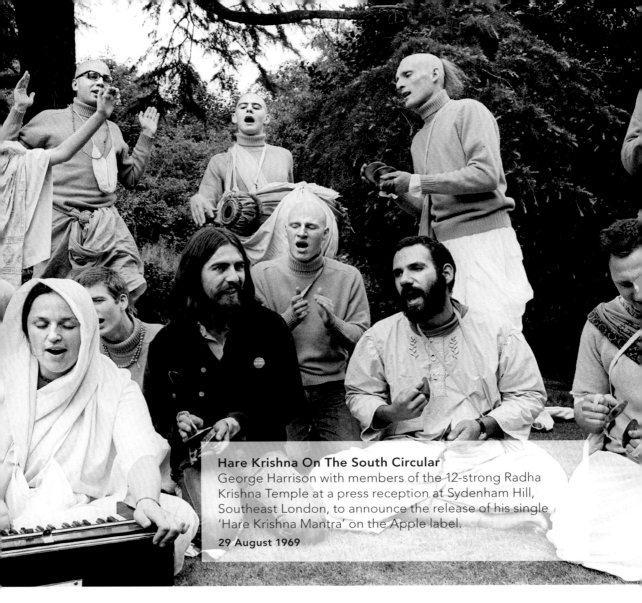

Hare Krishna On The South Circular
George Harrison with members of the 12-strong Radha Krishna Temple at a press reception at Sydenham Hill, Southeast London, to announce the release of his single 'Hare Krishna Mantra' on the Apple label.

29 August 1969

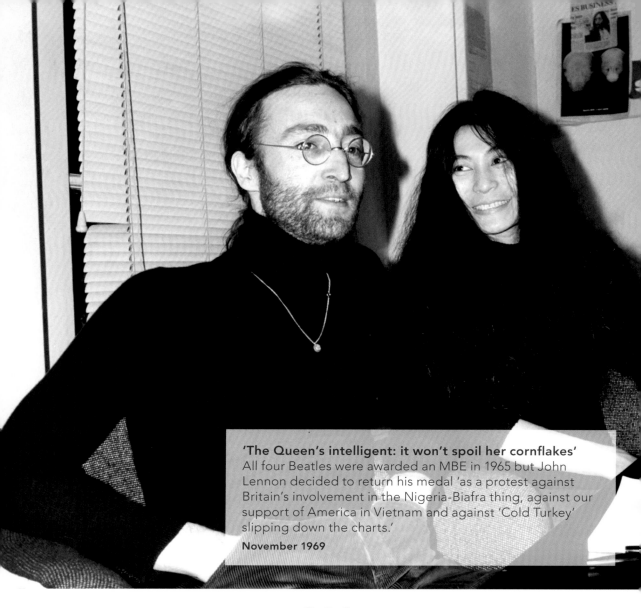

'The Queen's intelligent: it won't spoil her cornflakes'
All four Beatles were awarded an MBE in 1965 but John Lennon decided to return his medal 'as a protest against Britain's involvement in the Nigeria-Biafra thing, against our support of America in Vietnam and against 'Cold Turkey' slipping down the charts.'
November 1969

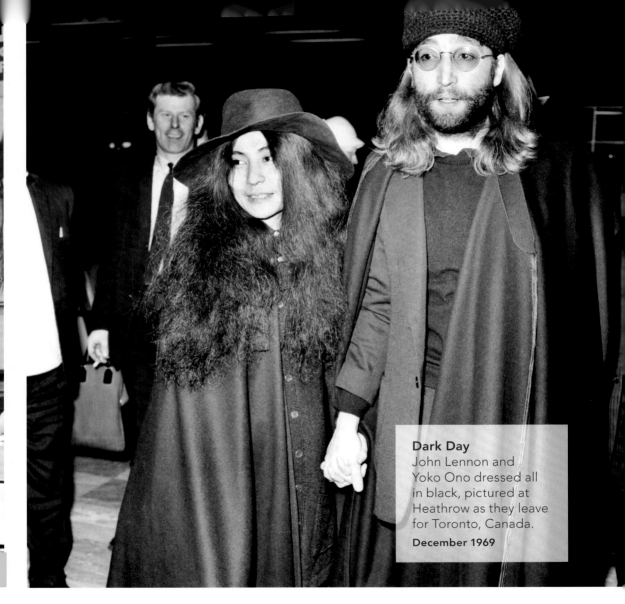

Dark Day
John Lennon and
Yoko Ono dressed all
in black, pictured at
Heathrow as they leave
for Toronto, Canada.
December 1969

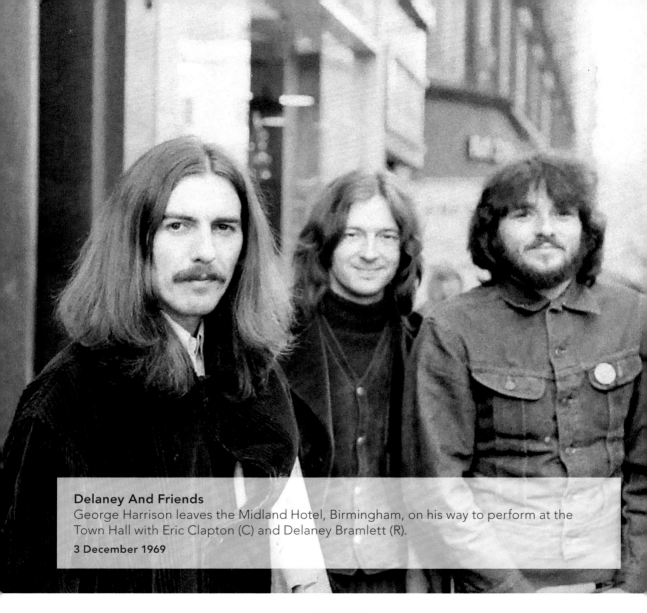

Delaney And Friends
George Harrison leaves the Midland Hotel, Birmingham, on his way to perform at the Town Hall with Eric Clapton (C) and Delaney Bramlett (R).

3 December 1969

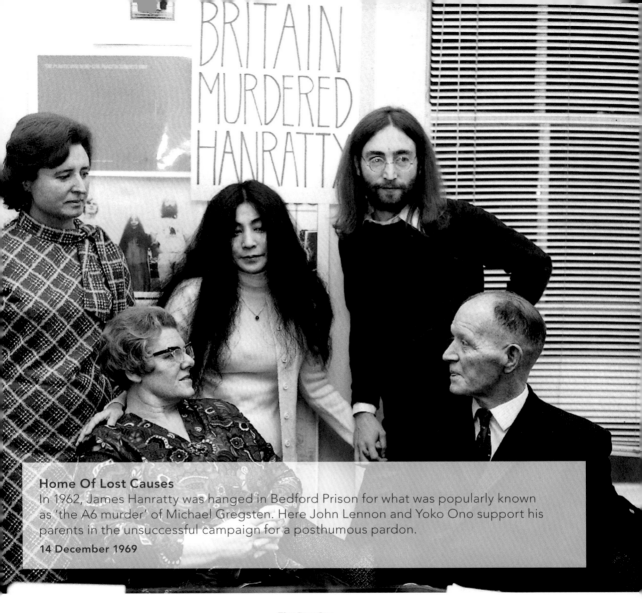

Home Of Lost Causes

In 1962, James Hanratty was hanged in Bedford Prison for what was popularly known as 'the A6 murder' of Michael Gregsten. Here John Lennon and Yoko Ono support his parents in the unsuccessful campaign for a posthumous pardon.

14 December 1969

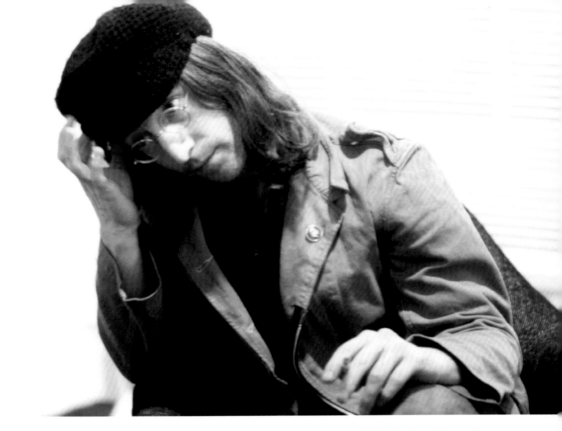

It's All In Here

John Lennon in somewhat pensive mood.

1970

Hair Today, Gone Tomorrow

John Lennon and Yoko Ono pictured on the roof of Black House, a Black Power commune in Holloway Road, North London, to which they donated a sack full of their hair for a fund-raising auction. With them is Michael X, the first man to be imprisoned in Britain under the Race Relations Act, who was later convicted of murder in Guyana and hanged in 1975.

4 February 1970

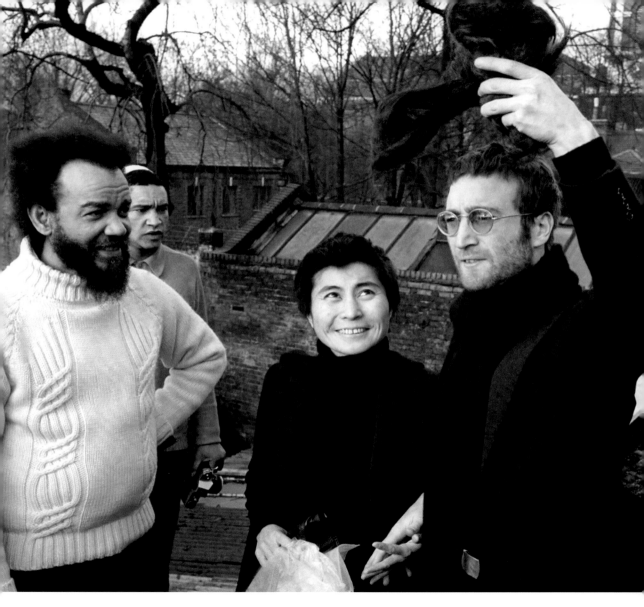

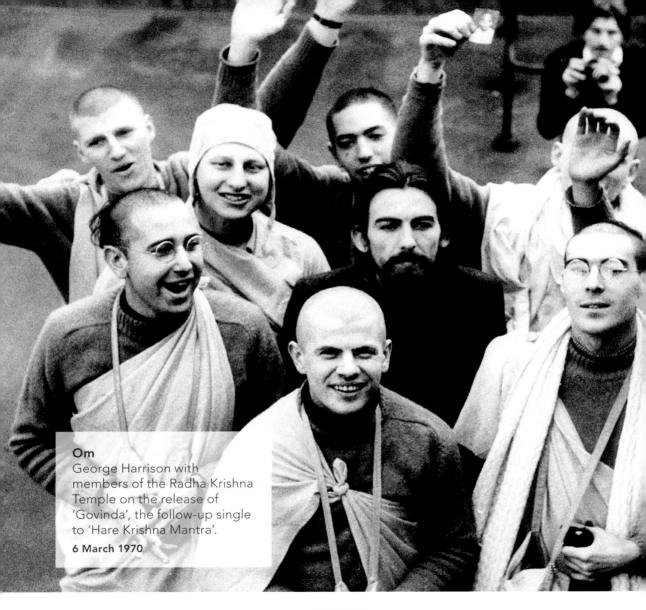

Om
George Harrison with members of the Radha Krishna Temple on the release of 'Govinda', the follow-up single to 'Hare Krishna Mantra'.

6 March 1970

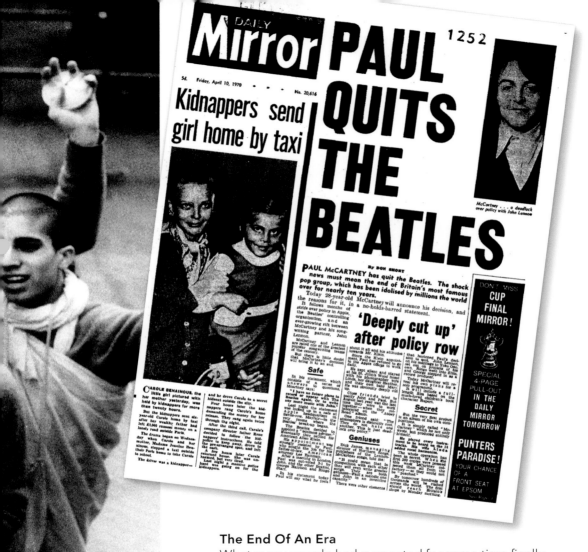

The End Of An Era
What many people had suspected for some time finally became public: The Beatles were splitting up.

10 April 1970

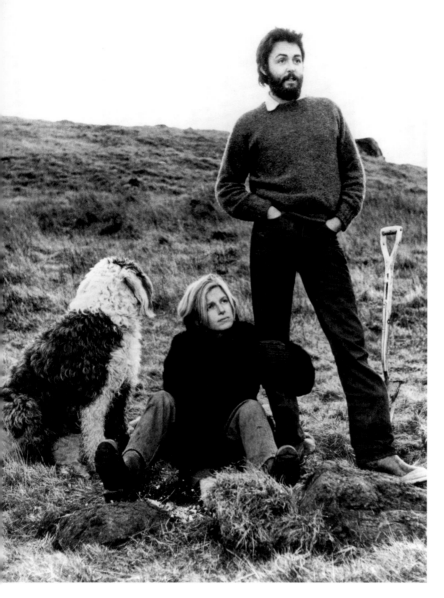

Spreading Wings

Paul McCartney finally married in 1969. His wife Linda (née Eastman) became increasingly involved in his music and joined him in his new band, Wings. Here they are with dog Ringo on their farm near Campbeltown, Scotland.

1971

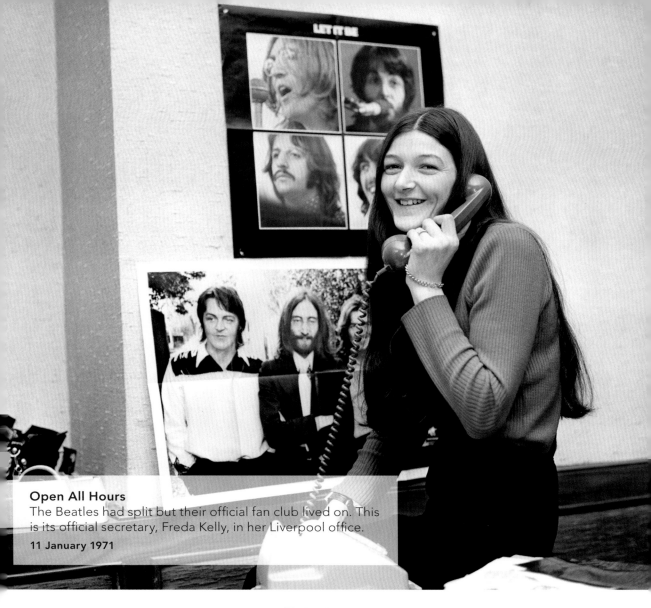

Open All Hours

The Beatles had split but their official fan club lived on. This is its official secretary, Freda Kelly, in her Liverpool office.

11 January 1971

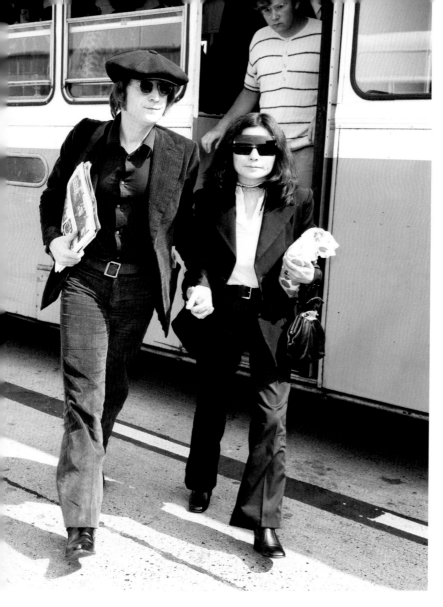

Holding Hands

John Lennon and Yoko Ono arrive back at London Heathrow Airport from the United States.

1 July 1971

RORing fire

Ringo Starr teamed up with furniture designer Robin Cruickshank to form a company named ROR (Ringo Or Robin) Ltd. This is one of their earliest creations, a fireplace that sold for £480.

13 September 1971

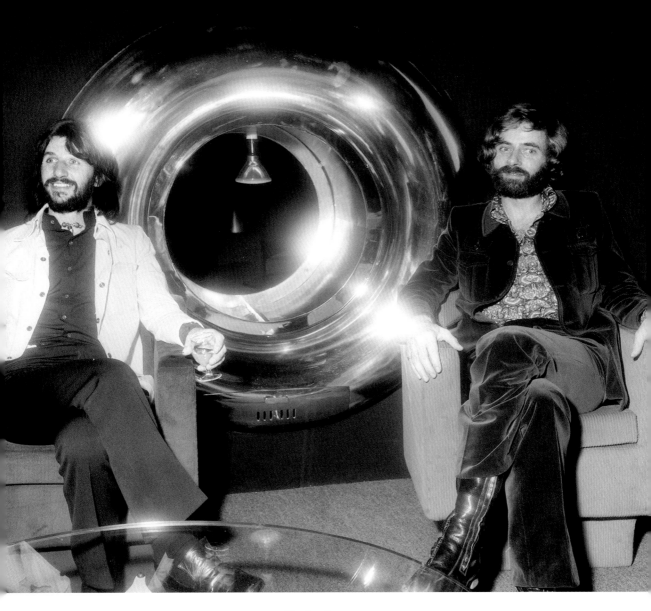

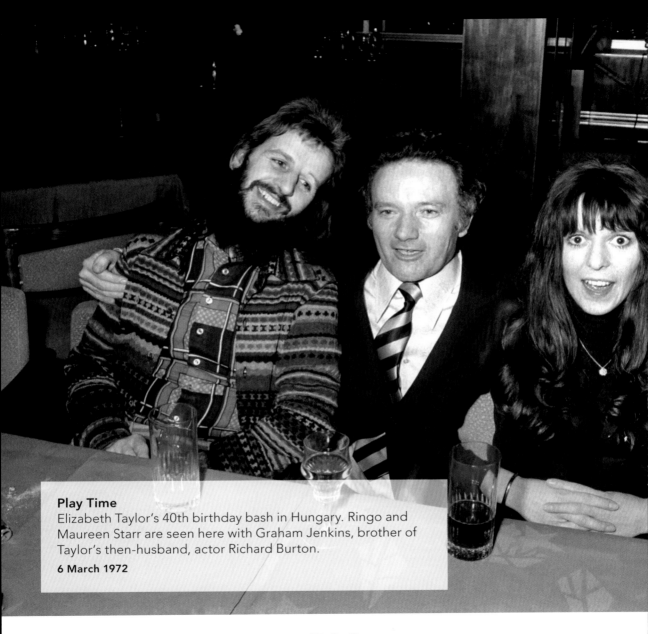

Play Time
Elizabeth Taylor's 40th birthday bash in Hungary. Ringo and
Maureen Starr are seen here with Graham Jenkins, brother of
Taylor's then-husband, actor Richard Burton.

6 March 1972

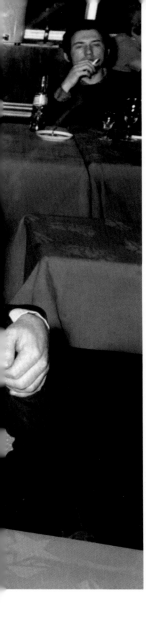

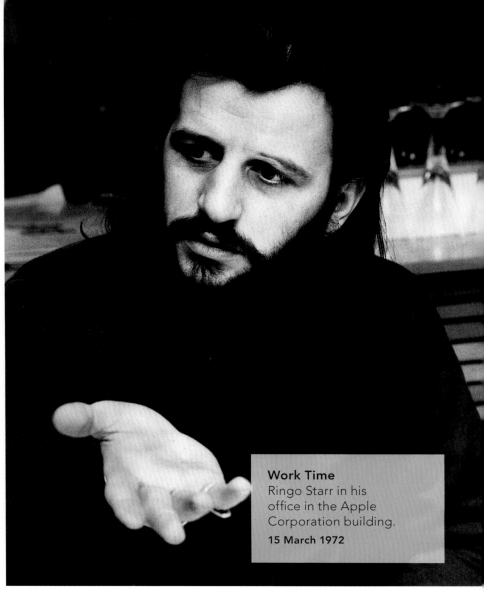

Work Time
Ringo Starr in his office in the Apple Corporation building.
15 March 1972

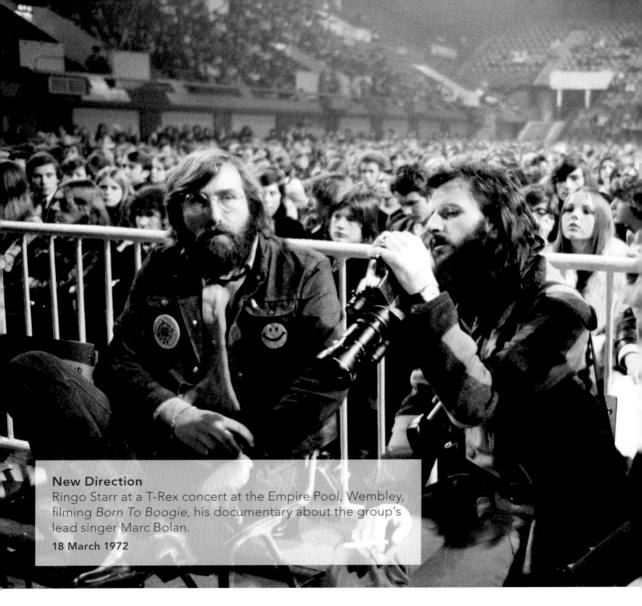

New Direction
Ringo Starr at a T-Rex concert at the Empire Pool, Wembley, filming *Born To Boogie*, his documentary about the group's lead singer Marc Bolan.

18 March 1972

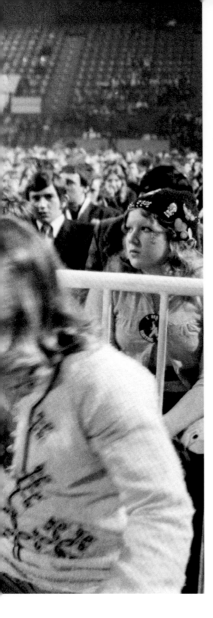

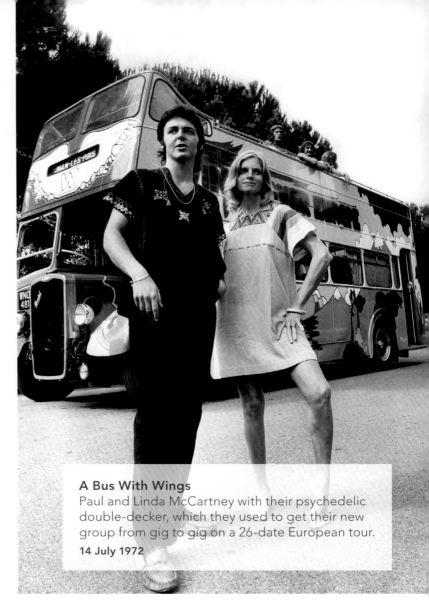

A Bus With Wings

Paul and Linda McCartney with their psychedelic double-decker, which they used to get their new group from gig to gig on a 26-date European tour.

14 July 1972

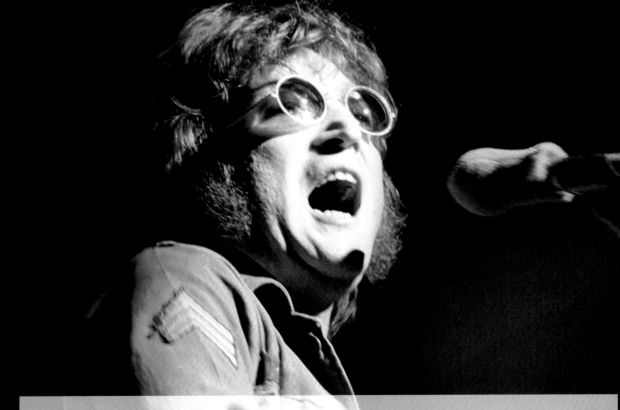

Last Concert
John Lennon and Yoko Ono on stage at New York's Madison Square Garden for one of two charity concerts on the same day in aid of the local Willowbrook School, a state-run institute for children with mental disabilities. These were Lennon's last full-scale performances in public.

30 August 1972

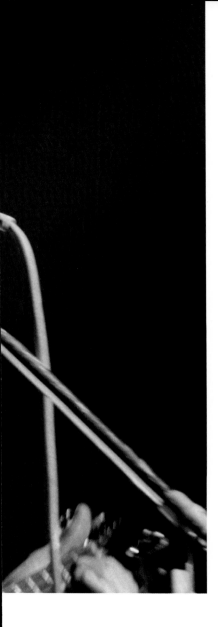

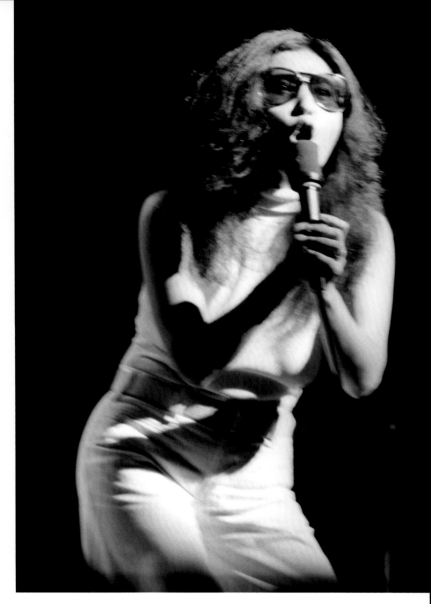

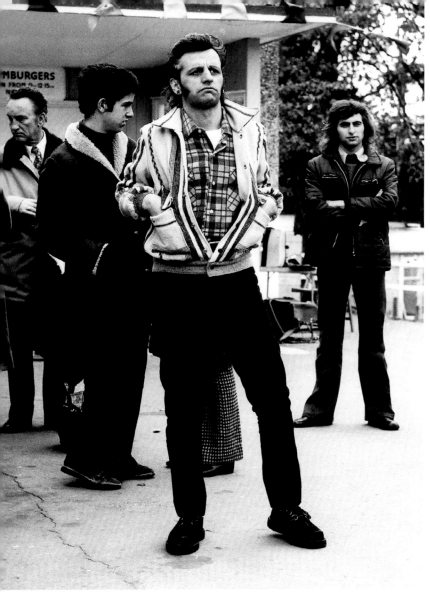

That'll Be The Day
Ringo Starr on location playing a Teddy boy in this 1973 film, which also starred David Essex and Billy Fury.

24 October 1972

Mixed Reception
A still from *That'll Be The Day*. The movie was panned by critics, but grossed more than £400,000.

1 February 1973

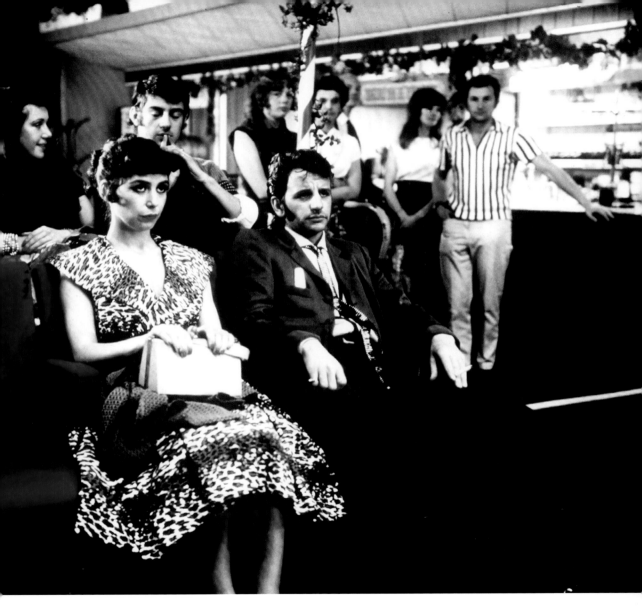

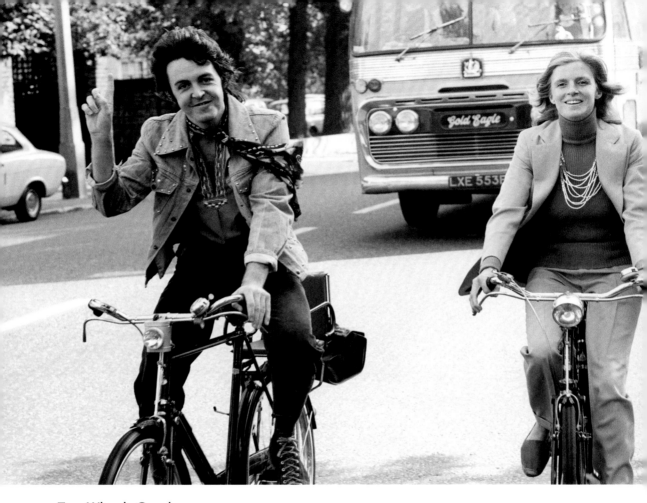

Two Wheels Good
Paul and Linda McCartney cycling round
London on an unseasonably sunny day.
6 February 1973

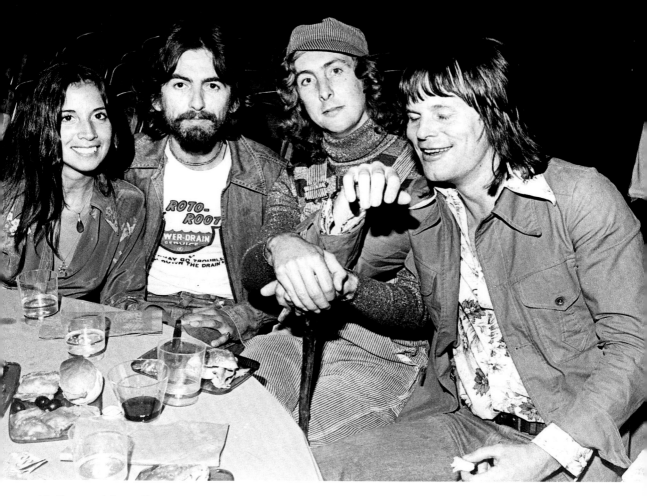

Hollywood Première

George Harrison with Olivia Arias, whom he later married, at the Hollywood première of *Monty Python and the Holy Grail*. With them are actor Eric Idle (second R) and the film's co-director Terry Gilliam.

18 July 1975

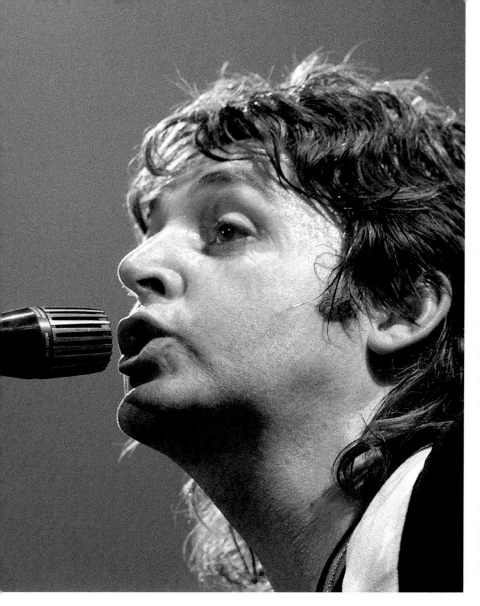
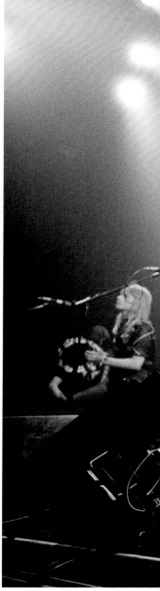

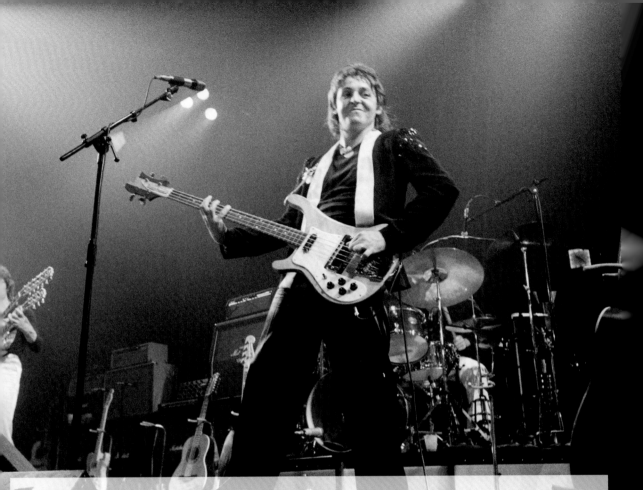

Quintet Set
Wings' line-up for the '76 tour comprised Paul and Linda McCartney, Jimmy McCulloch (L),
Denny Laine (C) and, hidden behind the drum kit, Joe English.
9 May 1976

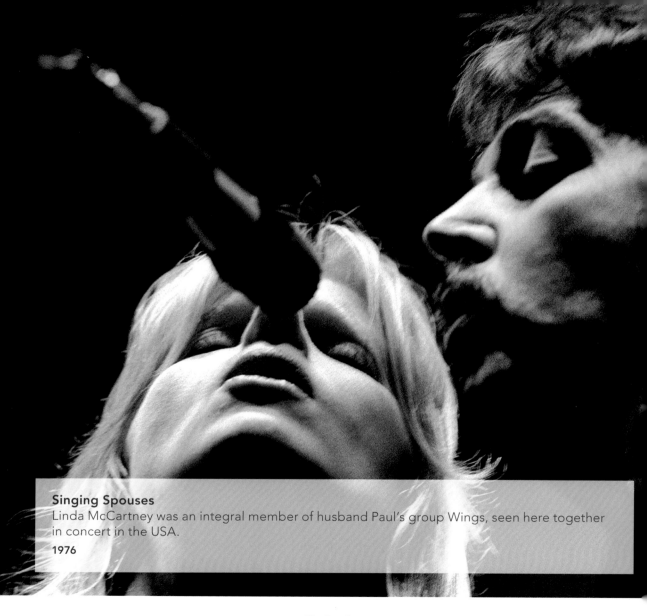

Singing Spouses
Linda McCartney was an integral member of husband Paul's group Wings, seen here together in concert in the USA.

1976

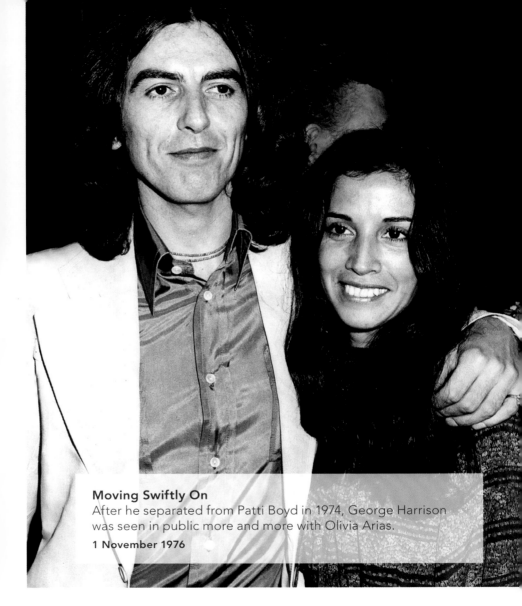

Moving Swiftly On
After he separated from Patti Boyd in 1974, George Harrison was seen in public more and more with Olivia Arias.

1 November 1976

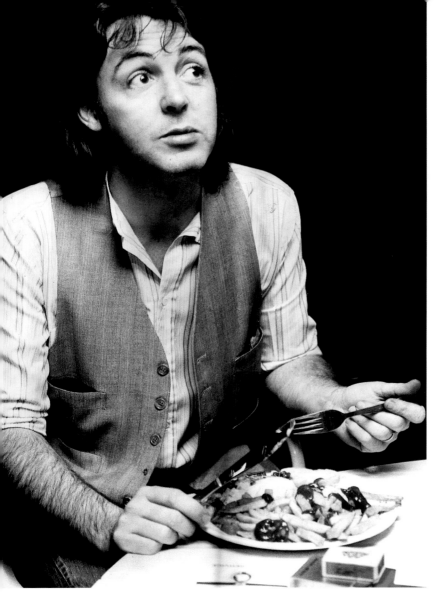

The Perfect Repast

Paul McCartney in a café eating fish and chips.

9 November 1977

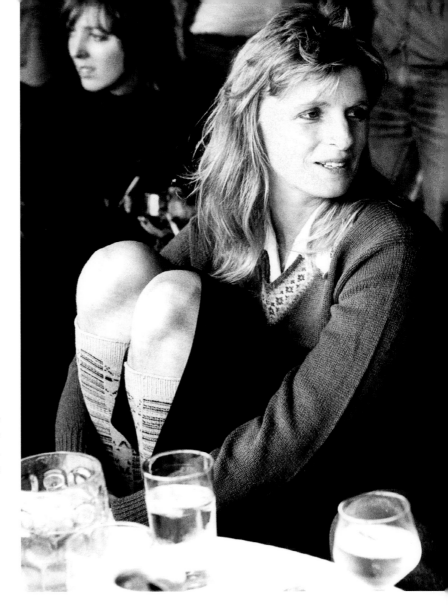

Linda McCartney
Linda McCartney
relaxes in a pub.

22 March 1978

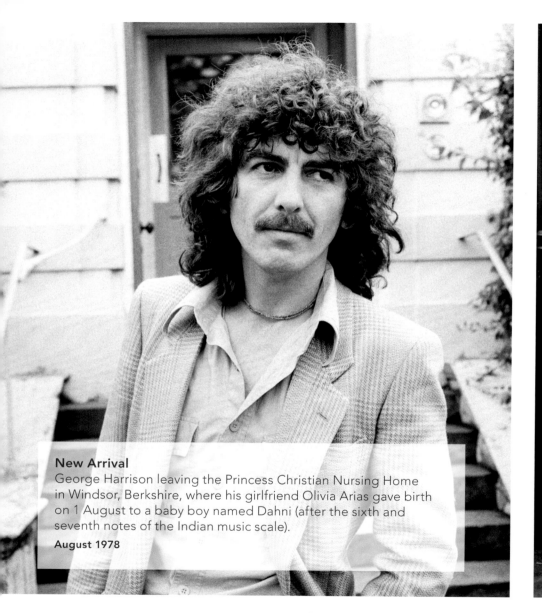

New Arrival
George Harrison leaving the Princess Christian Nursing Home in Windsor, Berkshire, where his girlfriend Olivia Arias gave birth on 1 August to a baby boy named Dahni (after the sixth and seventh notes of the Indian music scale).

August 1978

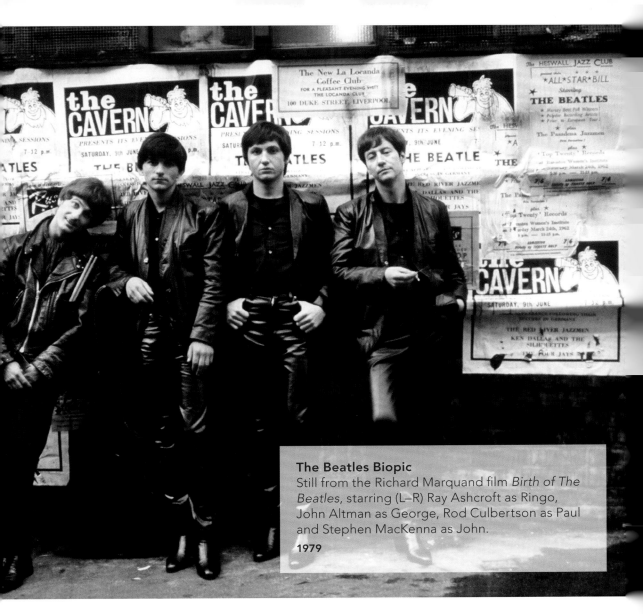

The Beatles Biopic
Still from the Richard Marquand film *Birth of The Beatles*, starring (L–R) Ray Ashcroft as Ringo, John Altman as George, Rod Culbertson as Paul and Stephen MacKenna as John.
1979

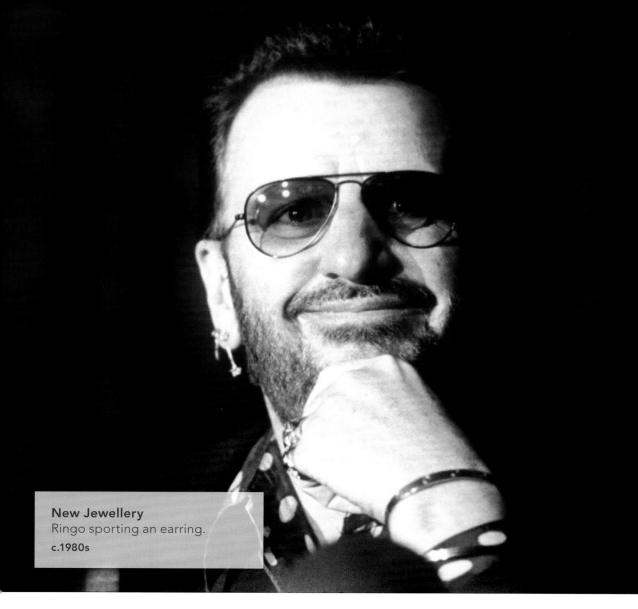

New Jewellery
Ringo sporting an earring.
c.1980s

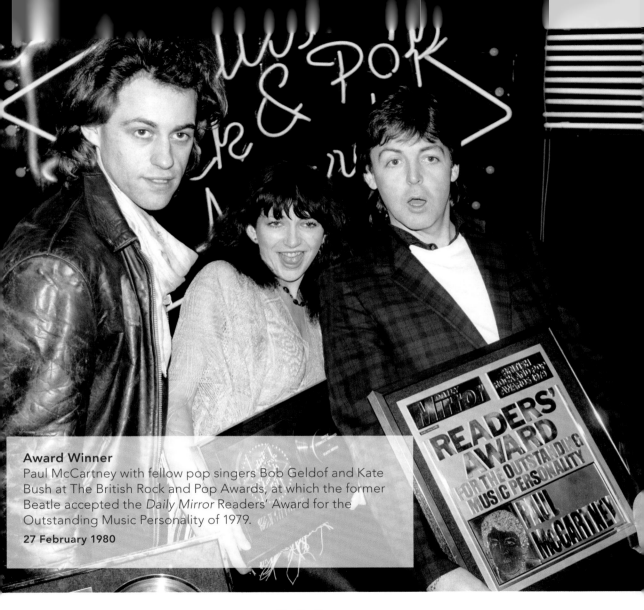

Award Winner
Paul McCartney with fellow pop singers Bob Geldof and Kate Bush at The British Rock and Pop Awards, at which the former Beatle accepted the *Daily Mirror* Readers' Award for the Outstanding Music Personality of 1979.

27 February 1980

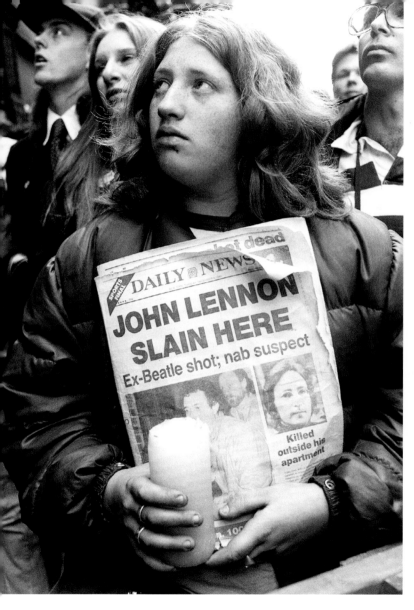

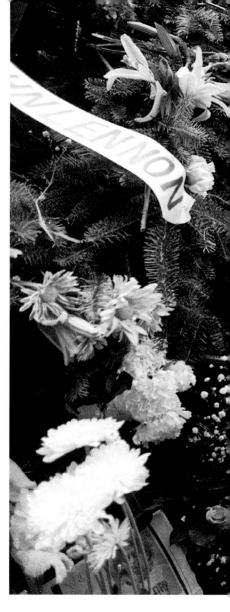

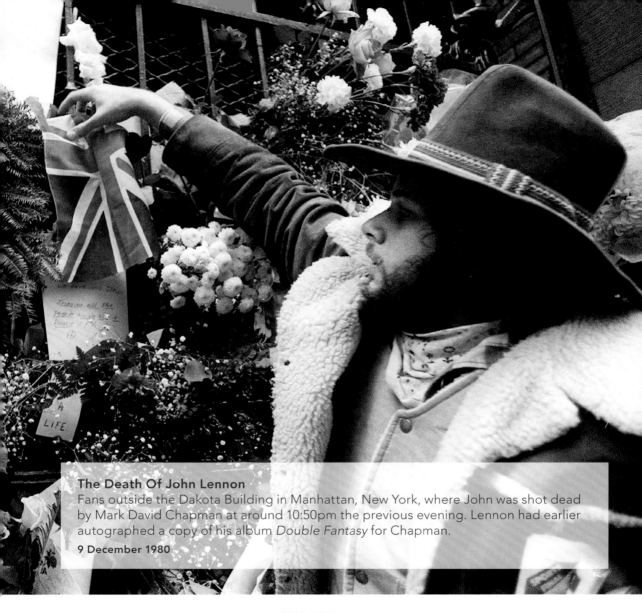

The Death Of John Lennon

Fans outside the Dakota Building in Manhattan, New York, where John was shot dead by Mark David Chapman at around 10:50pm the previous evening. Lennon had earlier autographed a copy of his album *Double Fantasy* for Chapman.

9 December 1980

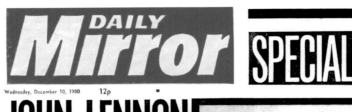

SPECIAL ISSUE

Wednesday, December 10, 1980   12p

JOHN LENNON
shot dead
in New York
Dec 8 1980
DEATH
OF A
HERO

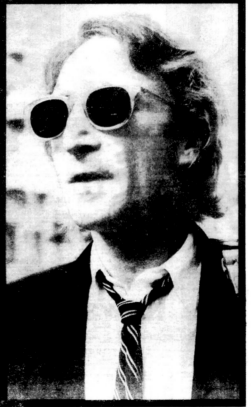

MURDERED SUPERSTAR: One of the last pictures of ex-Beatle John Lennon, taken in New York three weeks ago.

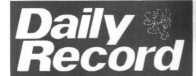

Daily Record

12p SCOTLAND'S BIGGEST DAILY SALE No. 26,589

FAREWELL TO JOHN LENNON

THE KISS

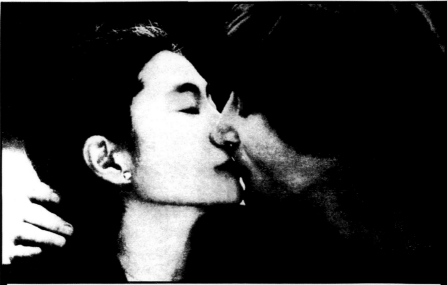

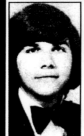

THE GUNMAN ...
Mark Chapman

AND THE KILLER

THIS picture, of John Lennon kissing his wife Yoko Ono, is how he will be remembered ... how he would want to be remembered.

For it sums up his tenderness, his love, his inner peace—his real nature hidden beneath the outward cynicism of his rebel image.

John liked the picture so much that he chose it for the cover of his latest record.

Tragically, it was partly because of that record that he died —gunned down at the age of 40 by a religious maniac who had earlier bought the album and got him to autograph it.

I'VE JUST SHOT JOHN LENNON

PAGES 2 AND 3

The Beatles
245

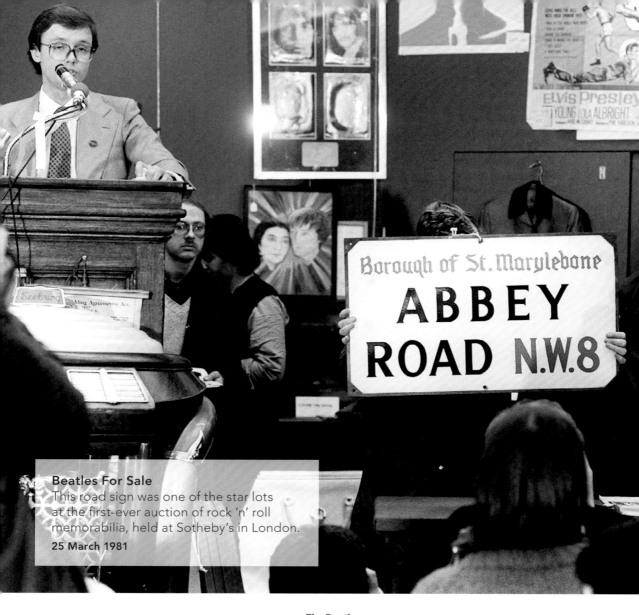

Beatles For Sale
This road sign was one of the star lots at the first-ever auction of rock 'n' roll memorabilia, held at Sotheby's in London.

25 March 1981

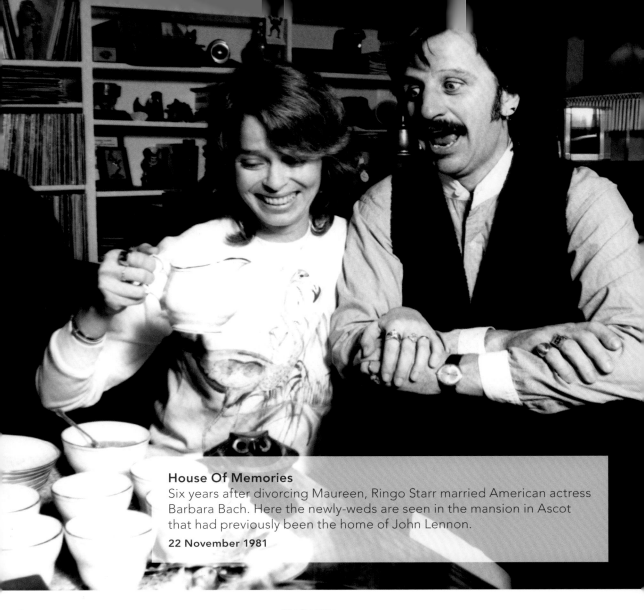

House Of Memories
Six years after divorcing Maureen, Ringo Starr married American actress
Barbara Bach. Here the newly-weds are seen in the mansion in Ascot
that had previously been the home of John Lennon.

22 November 1981

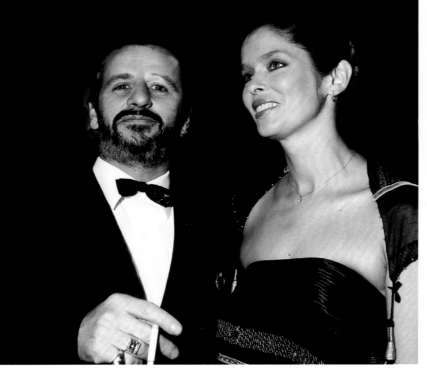

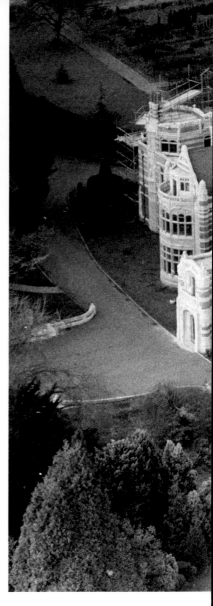

Inveterate Movie-goers
Ringo Starr and Barbara
Bach at the British première
of *Gandhi*, a film directed
by Richard Attenborough
and starring Ben Kingsley
in the title role.
2 December 1982

Crackerbox Palace
This was George Harrison's
affectionate name for Friar
Park, the 120-room neo-
Gothic mansion in Henley-on-
Thames, Oxfordshire, which
he bought in January 1970.
12 February 1984

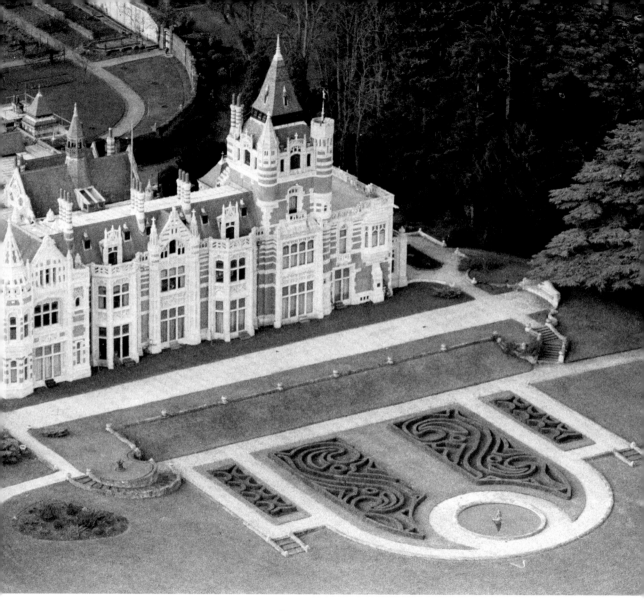

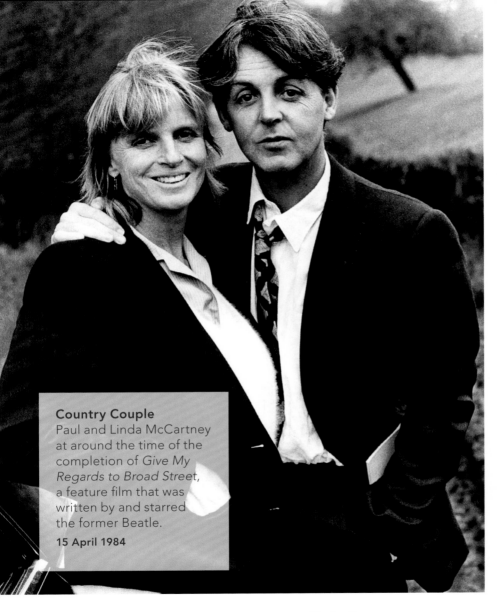
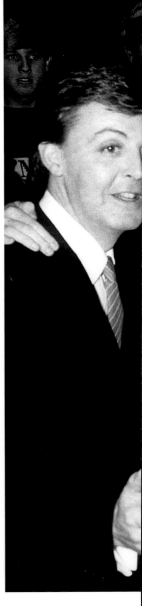

Country Couple
Paul and Linda McCartney at around the time of the completion of *Give My Regards to Broad Street*, a feature film that was written by and starred the former Beatle.

15 April 1984

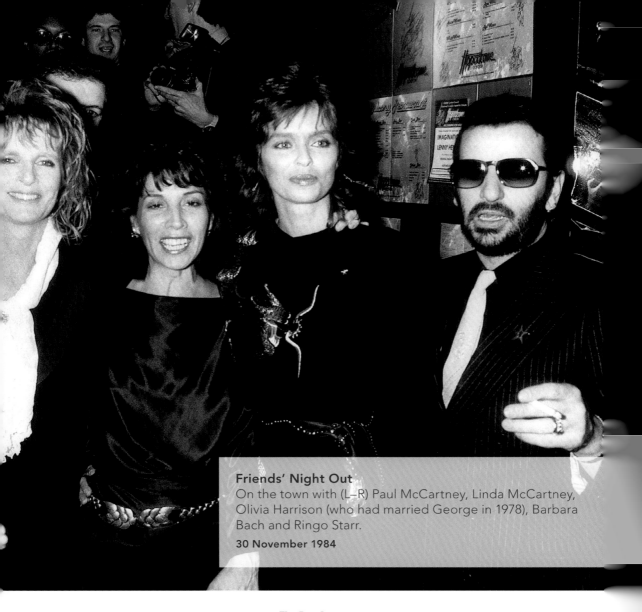

Friends' Night Out
On the town with (L–R) Paul McCartney, Linda McCartney, Olivia Harrison (who had married George in 1978), Barbara Bach and Ringo Starr.

30 November 1984

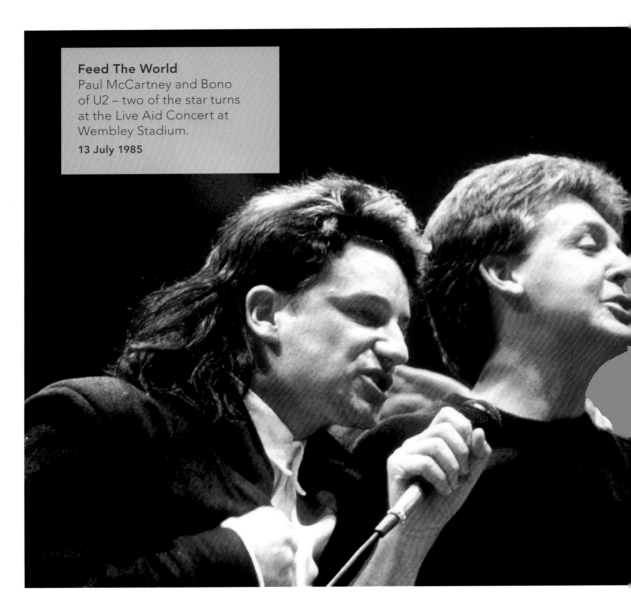

Feed The World
Paul McCartney and Bono of U2 – two of the star turns at the Live Aid Concert at Wembley Stadium.

13 July 1985

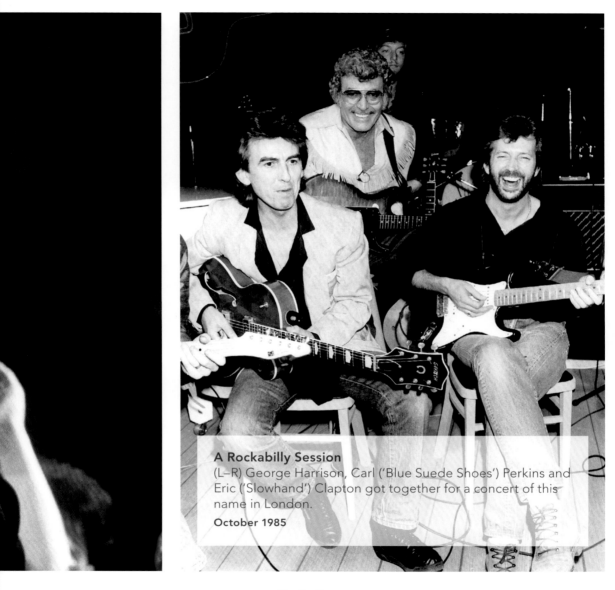

A Rockabilly Session
(L–R) George Harrison, Carl ('Blue Suede Shoes') Perkins and Eric ('Slowhand') Clapton got together for a concert of this name in London.
October 1985

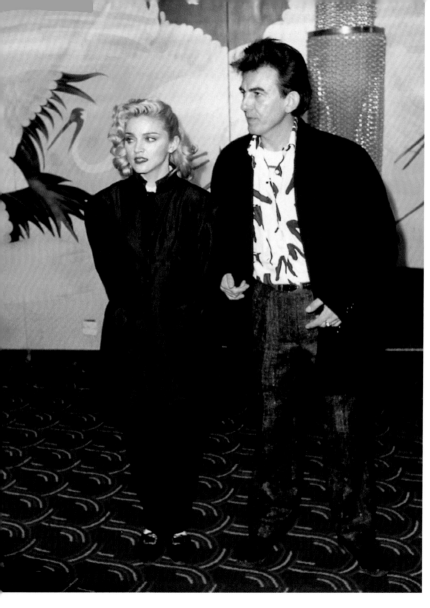

Material Girl
George Harrison with Madonna in the year of the release of the film *Shanghai Surprise*, which he produced and in which she starred.

March 1986

Posthumous Revelations
Cynthia Lennon hit the headlines when her account of life with John detailed his jealous rages and ill-treatment of their son Julian.

26 October 1988

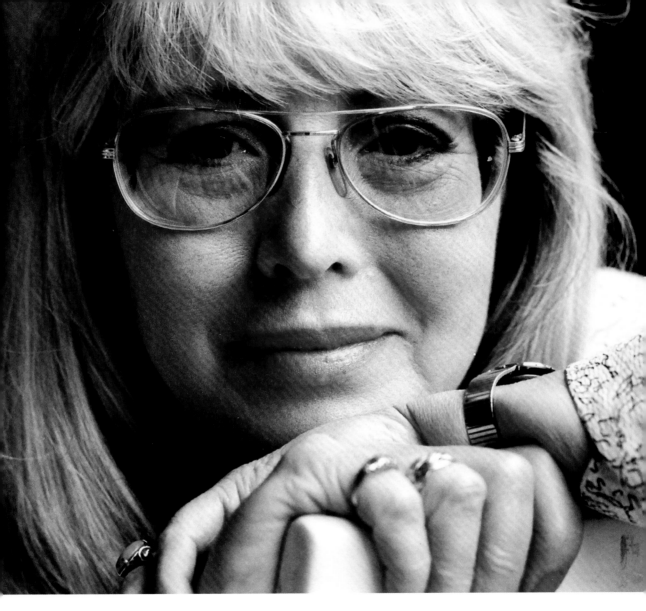

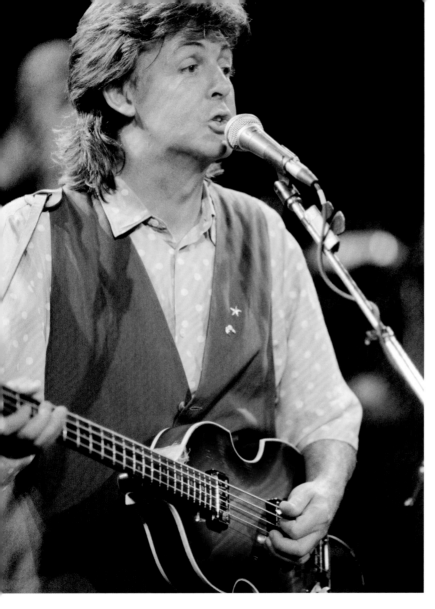

Old Songs

Paul McCartney performs live at London's Playhouse Theatre at the start of another world tour. This was the first time since The Beatles broke up that he had incorporated their material into his act.

27 July 1989

Summer Break

George, Olivia and Dhani Harrison at London Heathrow Airport.

2 August 1989

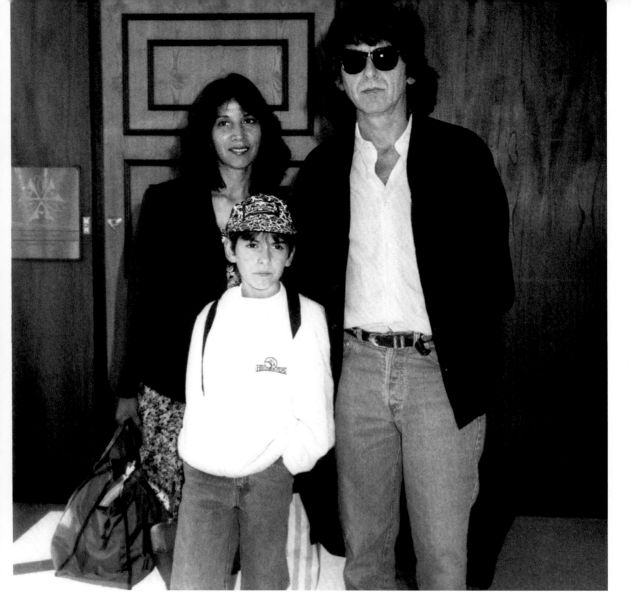

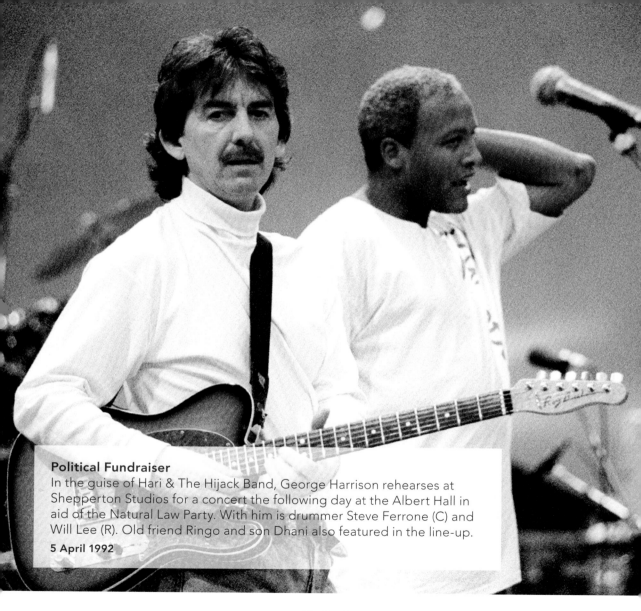

Political Fundraiser
In the guise of Hari & The Hijack Band, George Harrison rehearses at Shepperton Studios for a concert the following day at the Albert Hall in aid of the Natural Law Party. With him is drummer Steve Ferrone (C) and Will Lee (R). Old friend Ringo and son Dhani also featured in the line-up.

5 April 1992

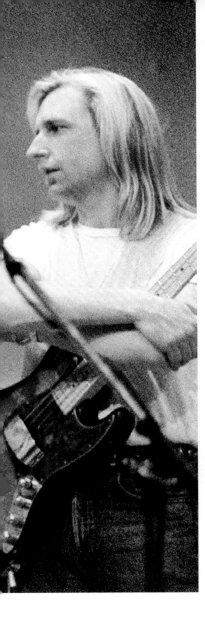

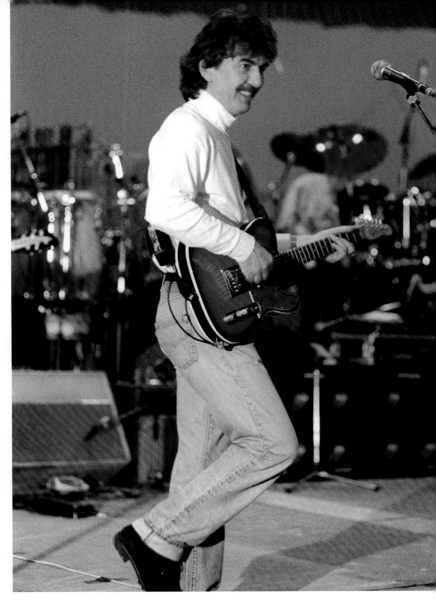

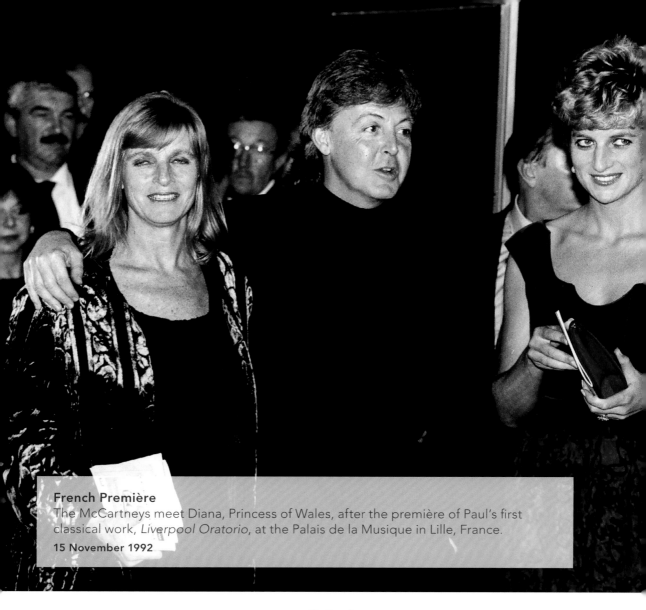

French Première
The McCartneys meet Diana, Princess of Wales, after the première of Paul's first classical work, *Liverpool Oratorio*, at the Palais de la Musique in Lille, France.

15 November 1992

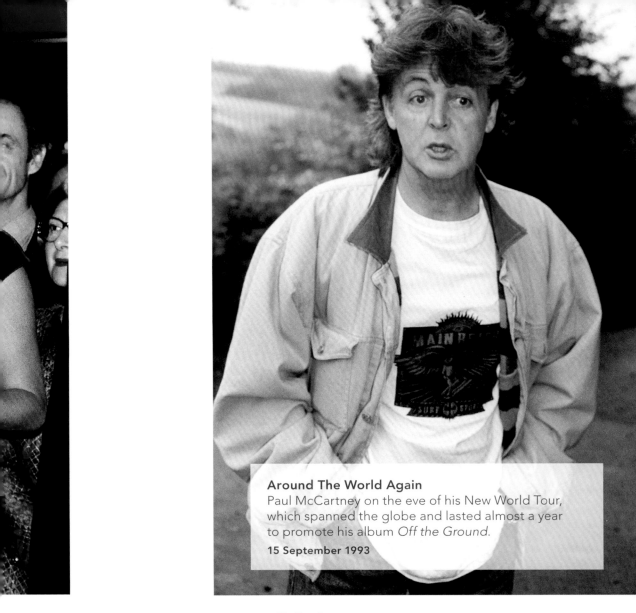

Around The World Again
Paul McCartney on the eve of his New World Tour, which spanned the globe and lasted almost a year to promote his album *Off the Ground*.

15 September 1993

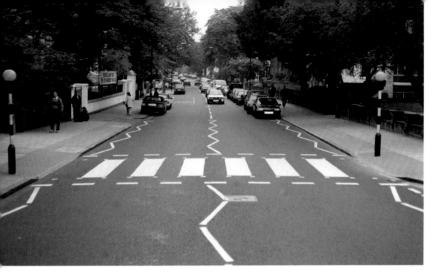

Abbey Road

The zebra crossing that appeared on the cover of *Abbey Road*, photographed almost exactly 25 years after the album's original release. Later it became not only the world's most famous pedestrian crossing but also one of the more dangerous, as motorists were faced almost daily with people imitating The Beatles.

25 September 1994

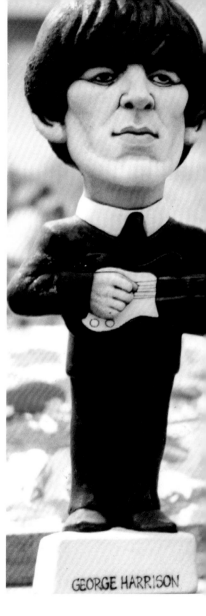

Clay Figures

Groggs are clay caricatures created by John Hughes of Pontypridd, Wales, depicting celebrities. These are among his best-selling lines.

November 1996

GEORGE HARRISON

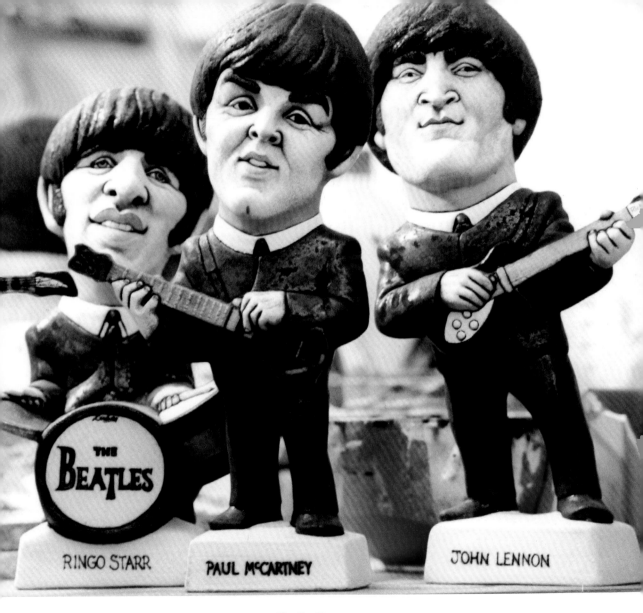

RINGO STARR   PAUL McCARTNEY   JOHN LENNON

The Beatles
263

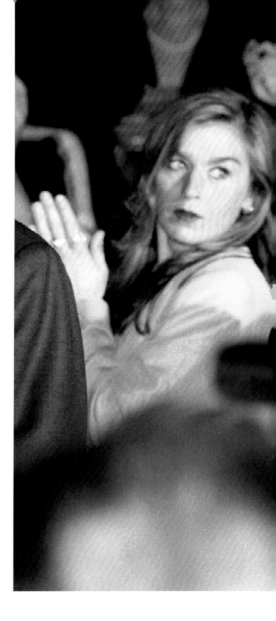

Designer Daughter
Paul and Linda McCartney
applaud their fashion designer
daughter Stella at the end of
her first show for Chloe in Paris.
Linda had been diagnosed
with breast cancer in 1995, and
passed away in April 1998.

15 October 1997

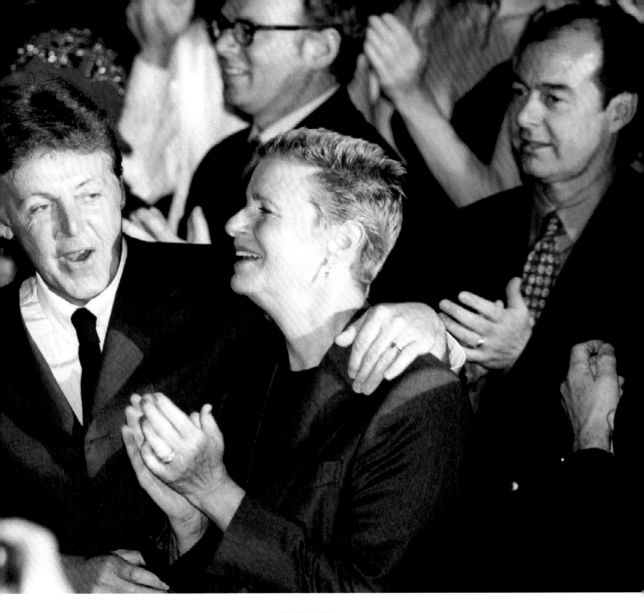

Death Of George Harrison
George Harrison died from lung cancer at the age of 58.
He was cremated and in a private ceremony his ashes were
scattered in the Ganges and Yamuna rivers in India.
29 November 2001

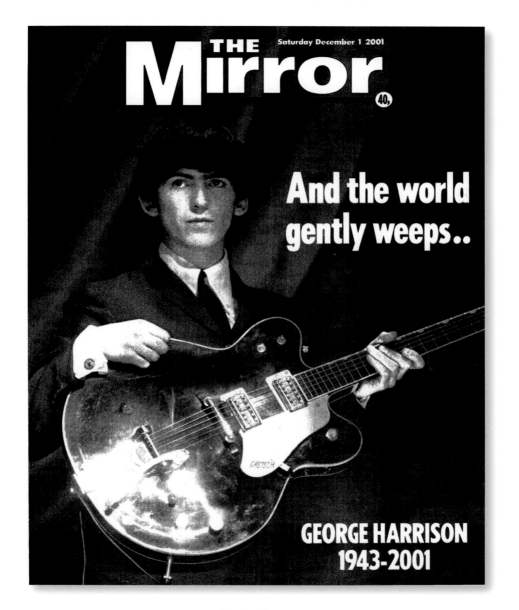

THE **Mirror** Saturday December 1 2001 40p

And the world gently weeps..

GEORGE HARRISON
1943-2001

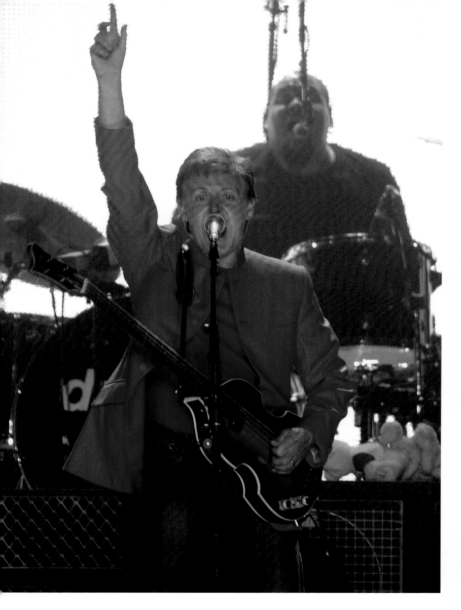
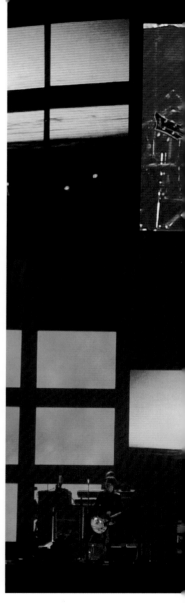

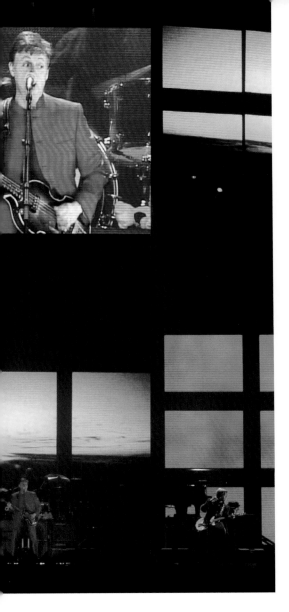

Live In Sheffield

Paul McCartney plays live on stage at the Hallam FM Arena at the start of his Back In The World tour.

6 April 2003

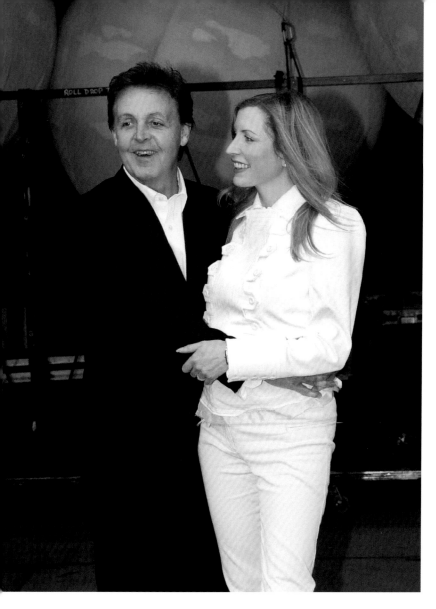

Married Man

Paul McCartney married Heather Mills on 11 June 2002. Today the couple announced that they are expecting their first child.

29 May 2003

Blooming In Glasgow

Paul and Heather Mills McCartney, the latter now visibly pregnant, at Prestwick Airport. Their daughter, Beatrice Milly, was born on 28 October 2003.

2003

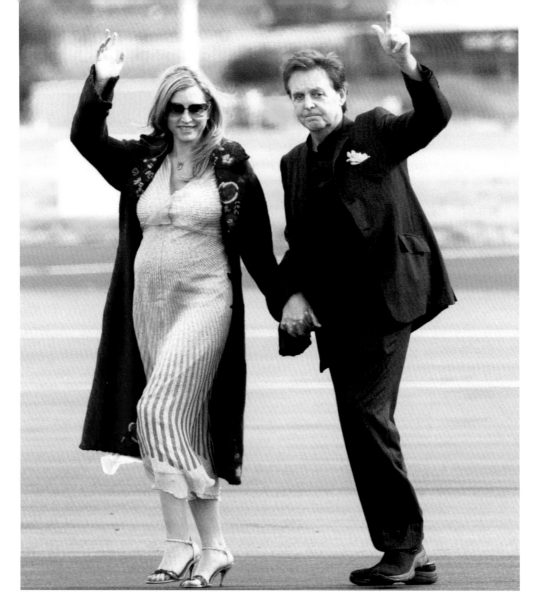

The Beatles

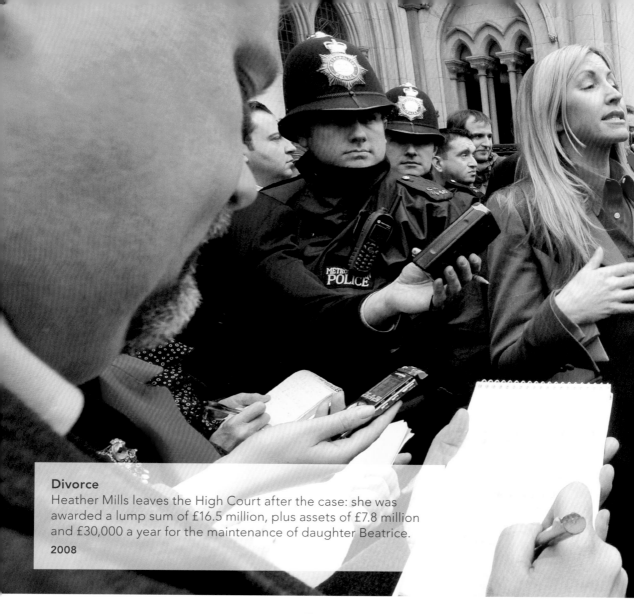

Divorce
Heather Mills leaves the High Court after the case: she was awarded a lump sum of £16.5 million, plus assets of £7.8 million and £30,000 a year for the maintenance of daughter Beatrice.
2008

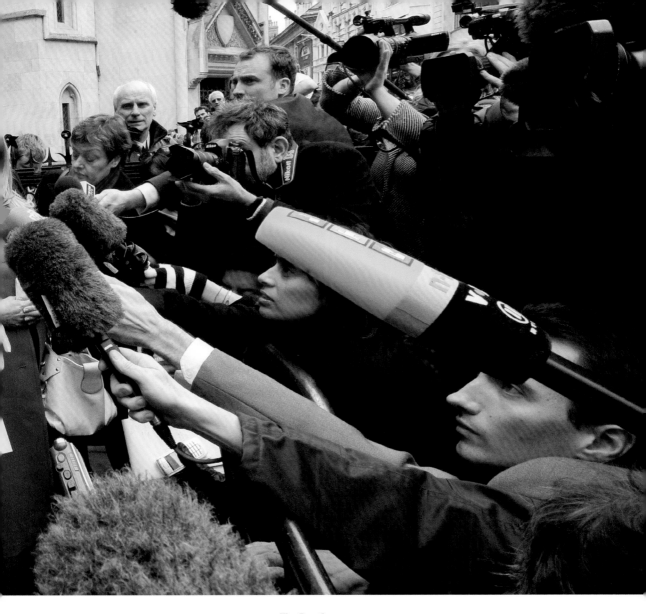

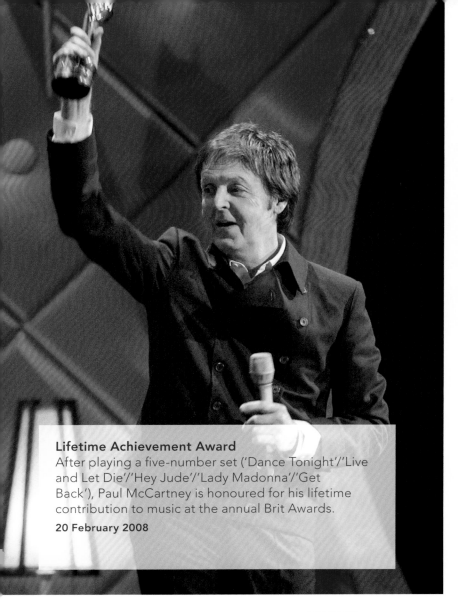
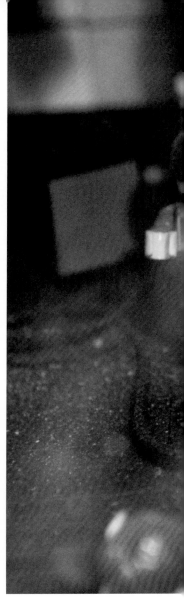

Lifetime Achievement Award
After playing a five-number set ('Dance Tonight'/'Live and Let Die'/'Hey Jude'/'Lady Madonna'/'Get Back'), Paul McCartney is honoured for his lifetime contribution to music at the annual Brit Awards.

20 February 2008

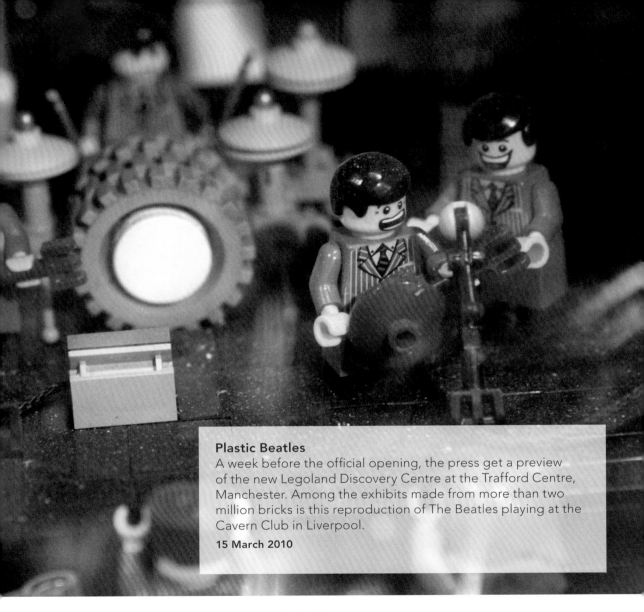

Plastic Beatles
A week before the official opening, the press get a preview of the new Legoland Discovery Centre at the Trafford Centre, Manchester. Among the exhibits made from more than two million bricks is this reproduction of The Beatles playing at the Cavern Club in Liverpool.

15 March 2010

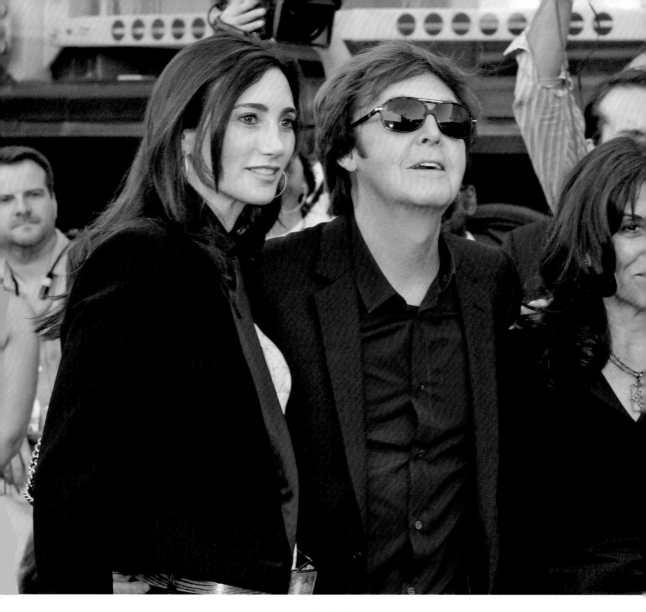

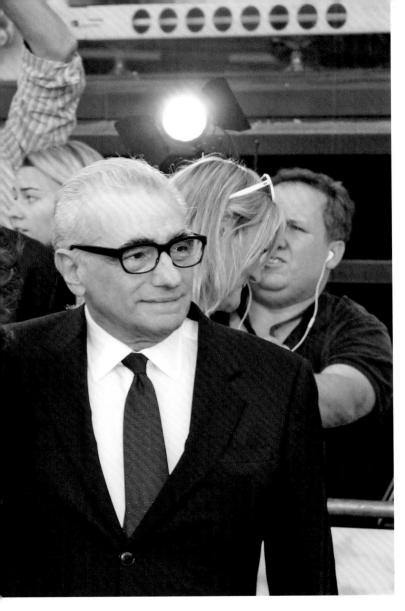

Scorsese Score
(L–R) Nancy Shevell, Paul McCartney, Olivia Harrison and Martin Scorsese at the London première of *George Harrison: Living in the Material World*.
2 October 2011

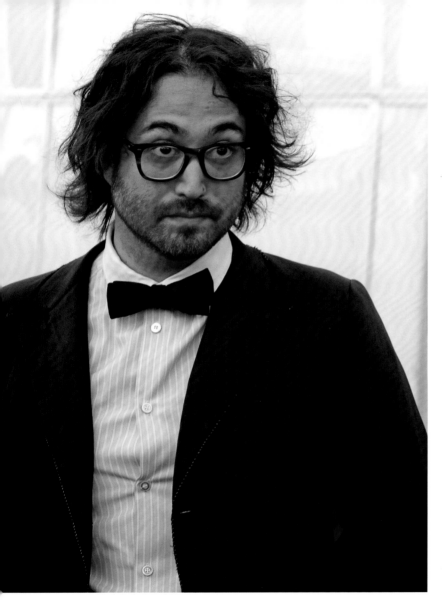

Lennon's Lad
Sean Lennon, singer, songwriter, musician and actor, and the only child of John Lennon and Yoko Ono, was among the guests at the première of the Scorsese biopic.
2 October 2011

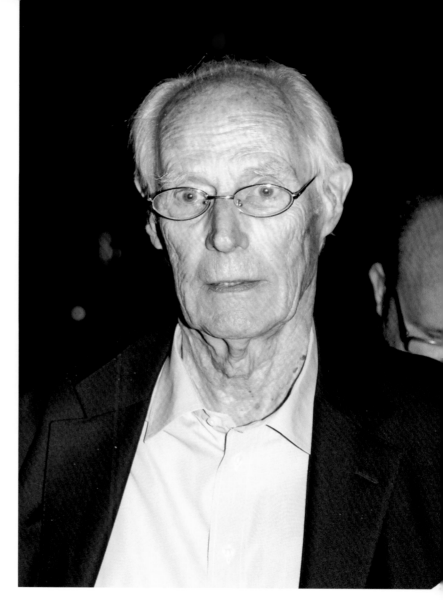

The Producer

Producer of much of The Beatles' best work, George Martin is among the honoured guests at the London première of *George Harrison: Living in the Material World*.

2 October 2011

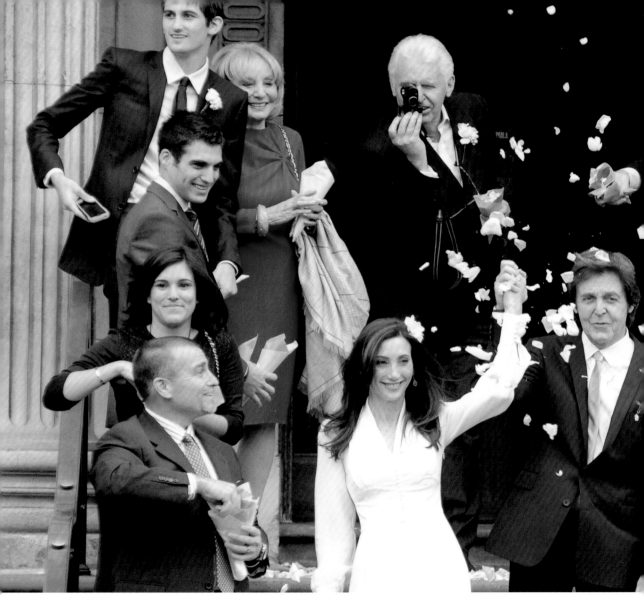

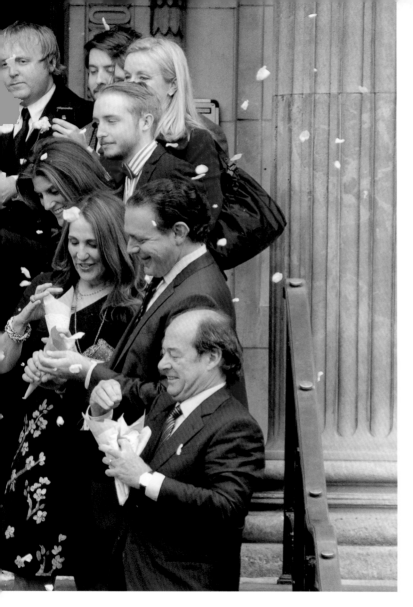

Third Time Lucky
At the start of his third marriage, Paul McCartney and new bride Nancy Shevell leave Old Marylebone Town Hall after their wedding ceremony.

9 October 2011

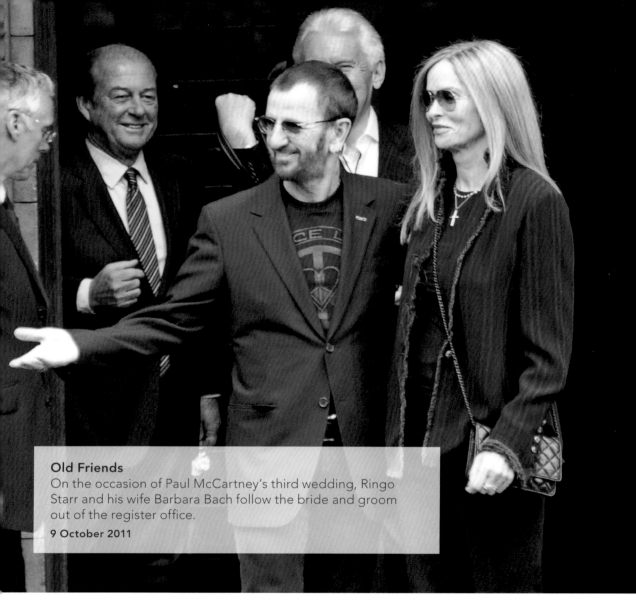

Old Friends

On the occasion of Paul McCartney's third wedding, Ringo Starr and his wife Barbara Bach follow the bride and groom out of the register office.

9 October 2011

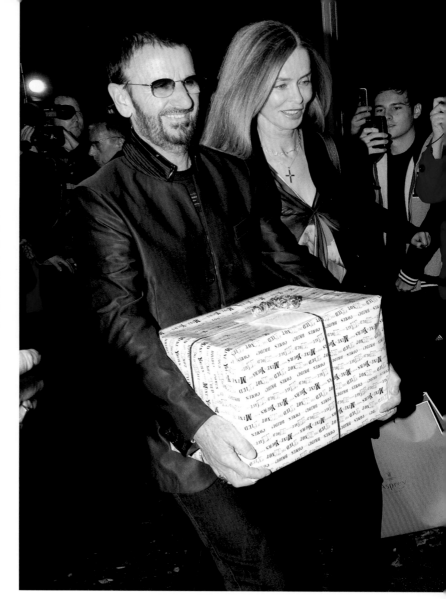

Wedding Present
Ringo Starr and Barbara
Bach on their way into
Paul McCartney's house in
Cavendish Avenue, St John's
Wood, London. The party went
on so late that the neighbours
complained about the noise.

9 October 2011

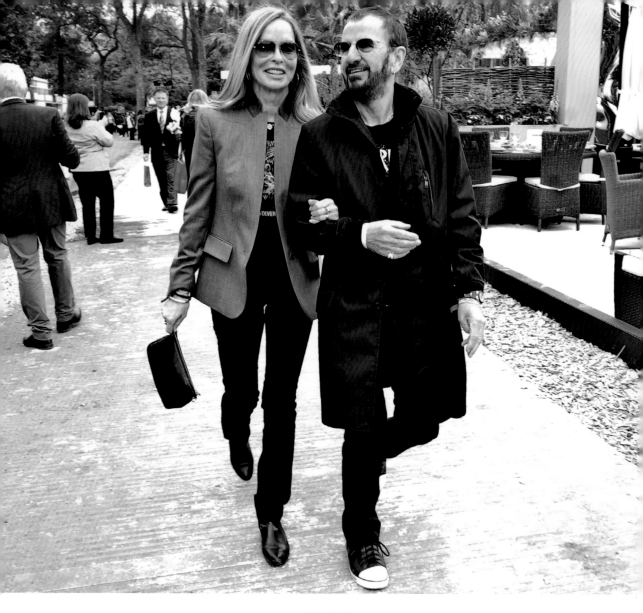

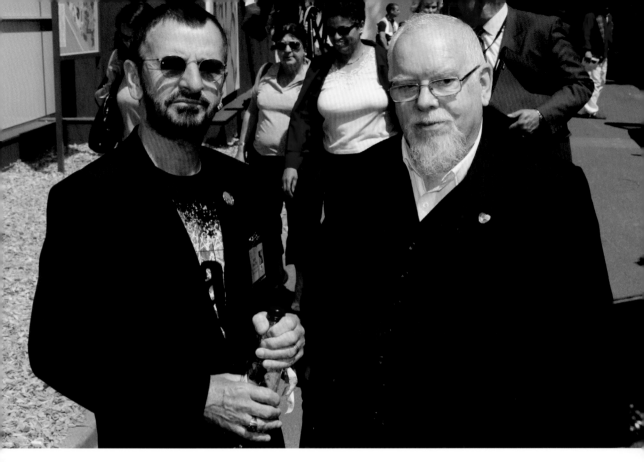

Chelsea Flower Show
Ringo Starr and Barbara Bach attend
the press and VIP preview day for the
annual Chelsea Flower Show at the
Royal Hospital Chelsea, London.

21 May 2012

Lonely Hearts' reunion
At the Chelsea Flower show,
Ringo ran into Peter Blake,
the artist who designed the
Sergeant Pepper album sleeve.

21 May 2012

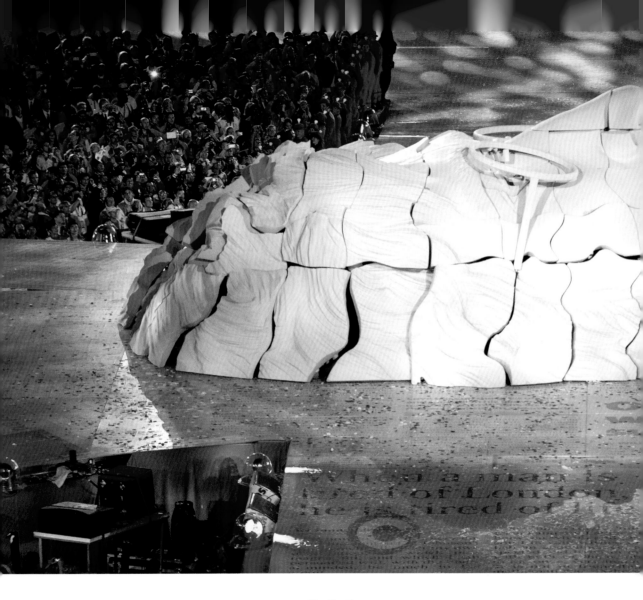

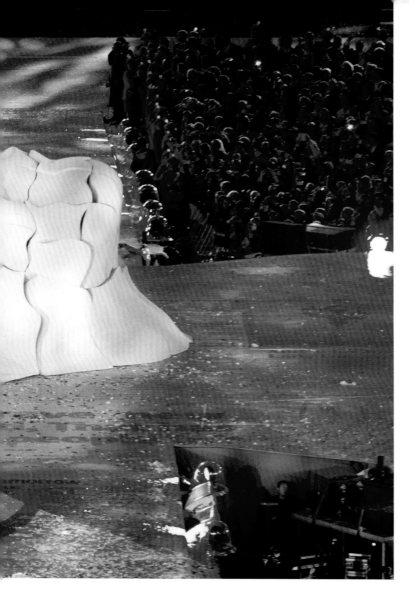

London Olympics

The Closing Ceremony of the 2012 London Olympics featured a sculpture in the shape of the late John Lennon that was formed onstage, along with video footage of the star singing *Imagine*: a poignant tribute to the Beatle who was cut off in his prime.

12 August 2012

The publishers gratefully acknowledge Mirrorpix, from whose extensive archives
the photographs in this book have been selected.

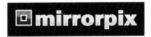

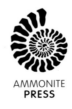

AMMONITE
PRESS